A Pocket Handbook
for the Dragon

A Pocket Handbook
for the
Dragon

**Peter Gerrard
&
Danny Doyle**

Duckworth

First published in 1984 by
Gerald Duckworth & Co. Ltd.
The Old Piano Factory
43 Gloucester Crescent, London NW1

© 1984 by Peter Gerrard

ISBN 0 7156 1788 5

British Library Cataloguing in Publication Data

Gerrard, Peter
  A pocket handbook for the Dragon.
  — (Duckworth home computing)
  1. Dragon 32 (Computer)
  I. Title
  001.64'04 QA76.8.D7

ISBN 0-7156-1788-5

Cover design: The Tab and the Arcuate stitching
pattern are, when applied to a pair of jeans, the trade
mark of Levi Strauss & Co., San Francisco, U.S.A.

Printed in Great Britain by
Redwood Burn Ltd., Trowbridge
and bound by Pegasus Bookbinding, Melksham

Contents

Preface

This book is a collection of relevant facts and figures for your Dragon 32 computer. Owing to the way the Dragon 64 has been designed, a lot of this will apply to that newer model as well.

In addition to memory maps, microprocessor instruction set, detailed notes on the available (and unavailable and undocumented) graphics pages, BASIC commands, error messages (again a few that you won't find in the Dragon manual but which none the less exist), and more, this book contains just about any fact or figure about the Dragon that you'll ever need to know.

In response to helpful suggestions from others (including Peter Worlock: thank you!), this handbook includes more than just facts and figures. At the end of the book there is an eight-page collection of useful hints and tips that make use of some of the material contained in the rest of the book. This should make the information contained here that little bit more accessible.

We'd like to thank anyone who, directly or indirectly, has contributed material to us. As ever, your comments are most welcome.

P.G. and D.D.

ASCII tables

Standard ASCII characters (7-bit code)

LSD	MSD	0	1	2	3	4	5	6	7
		000	001	010	011	100	101	110	111
0	0000	NUL	DLE	SP	0	@	P	‒	p
1	0001	SOH	DC1	!	1	A	Q	a	q
2	0010	STX	DC2	"	2	B	R	b	r
3	0011	ETX	DC3	£	3	C	S	c	s
4	0100	EOT	DC4	$	4	D	T	d	t
5	0101	ENQ	NAK	%	5	E	U	e	u
6	0110	ACK	SYN	&	6	F	V	f	v
7	0111	BEL	ETB	'	7	G	W	g	w
8	1000	BS	CAN	(	8	H	X	h	x
9	1001	HT	EM	)	9	I	Y	i	y
A	1010	LF	SUB	*	:	J	Z	j	z
B	1011	VT	ESC	+	;	K	[	k	
C	1100	FF	FS	,	<	L		l	
D	1101	CR	GS	‒	=	M		m	
E	1110	SO	RS	.	>	N		n	
F	1111	SI	US	/	?	O		o	DEL

The ASCII symbols.

NUL	– Null	DLE	– Data Link Escape
SOH	– Start of Heading	DC	– Device Control
STX	– Start of Text	NAK	– Negative Acknowledge
ETX	– End of Text	SYN	– Synchronous Idle
EOT	– End of Transmission	ETB	– End of Transmission Block
ENQ	– Enquiry	CAN	– Cancel
ACK	– Acknowledge	EM	– End of Medium
BEL	– Bell (audible alert)	SUB	– Substitute
BS	– Backspace	ESC	– Escape
HT	– Horizontal Tabulation	FS	– File Separator
LF	– Line Feed	GS	– Group Separator
VT	– Vertical Tabulation	RS	– Record Separator
FF	– Form Feed	US	– Unit Separator
CR	– Carriage Return	SP	– Space (Blank)
SO	– Shift Out	DEL	– Delete
SI	– Shift In		

Keyboard CNTL Sequences.

NUL - CNTL 1   DLE   - CNTL P
SOH - CNTL A   DC1/2/3/4 - CNTL Q/R/S/T
STX - CNTL B   NAK   - CNTL U
ETX - CNTL C   SYN   - CNTL V
EOT - CNTL D   ETB   - CNTL W
ENQ - CNTL E   CAN   - CNTL X
ACK - CNTL F   EM   - CNTL Y
BEL - CNTL G   SUB   - CNTL Z
BS   - CNTL H/BS   ESC   - ESC
HT   - CNTL I/TAB   FS   - CNTL BACKSLASH
LF   - CNTL J/LF   GS   - CNTL '
VT   - CNTL K   RS   - CNTL =
FF   - CNTL L   US   - CNTL -
CR   - CNTL M/CR   SP   - Space
SO   - CNTL N   SI   - CNTL O

ASCII codes

```
               ASCII Codes for keys
               ====================
```

KEY	HEX #		DECIMAL #	
	Unshifted	Shifted	Unshifted	Shifted
BREAK	03	03	03	03
CLEAR	0C	—	12	—
ENTER	0D	0D	13	13
SPACE	20	—	32	—
!	21	—	33	—
"	22	—	34	—
#	23	—	35	—
$	24	—	36	—
%	25	—	37	—
&	26	—	38	—
'	27	—	39	—
(	28	—	40	—
)	29	—	41	—
*	2A	—	42	—
+	2B	—	43	—
,	2C	—	44	—
-	2D	—	45	—
.	2E	—	46	—
/	2F	—	47	—
0	30	12	48	12
1	31	—	49	—
2	32	—	50	—
3	33	—	51	—
4	34	—	52	—
5	35	—	53	—
6	36	—	54	—
7	37	—	55	—
8	38	—	56	—
9	39	—	57	—
:	3A	—	58	—
;	3B	—	59	—
<	3C	—	60	—
=	3D	—	61	—
>	3E	—	62	—
?	3F	—	63	—
@	40	13	64	19

```
=====================================================================
=      KEY           HEX #             DECIMAL #            =
---------------------------------------------------------------------
=                Unshifted   Shifted  Unshifted   Shifted   =
=====================================================================
=                                                            =
=       A           61          41        97          65     =
=       B           62          42        98          66     =
=       C           63          43        99          67     =
=       D           64          44       100          68     =
=       E           65          45       101          69     =
=       F           66          46       102          70     =
=       G           67          47       103          71     =
=       H           68          48       104          72     =
=       I           69          49       105          73     =
=       J           6A          4A       106          74     =
=       K           6B          4B       107          75     =
=       L           6C          4C       108          76     =
=       M           6D          4D       109          77     =
=       N           6E          4E       110          78     =
=       O           6F          4F       111          79     =
=       P           70          50       112          80     =
=       Q           71          51       113          81     =
=       R           72          52       114          82     =
=       S           73          53       115          83     =
=       T           74          54       116          84     =
=       U           75          55       117          85     =
=       V           76          56       118          86     =
=       W           77          57       119          87     =
=       X           78          58       120          88     =
=       Y           79          59       121          89     =
=       Z           7A          5A       122          90     =
=     [CU]          5E          5F        94          95     =
=     [CD]          0A          5B        10          91     =
=     [CL]          08          15         8          21     =
=     [CR]          09          5D         9          93     =
=====================================================================
```

Note : CU is the up-arrow key
       CD is the down-arrow key
       CL is the left-arrow key
       CR is the right-arrow key

Basic expressions

In Dragon Basic, numeric expressions are carried out with
the following priority.

1) Brackets   ()   gives expressions within
                         brackets higher priority.

2) Functions   see section on BASIC functions.

3) Arithmetic   exponentiation
   operators   -   negation
                  *   multiplication
                  /   division
                  +   addition
                  -      subtraction

4) Relational   =   is equal to
   operators   <>   not equal to
                  <   less than
                  >   greater than
                  <=   less than or equal to
                  >=   greater than or equal to

5) Logical
   operators

These, and the relational operators, return a value of (-1)
if the result of an expression is true, or (0) if it is
false.

NOT   X   NOTX

OR   X   Y   X OR Y

AND   X   Y   X AND Y

To set a particular bit in a memory location, and keep the
rest as they were, you must POKE (LOC),PEEK(LOC) OR X. X
must have one of the following values:

Value   Bit set
-----   -------

   1   0
   2   1
   4   2
   8   3
  16   4
  32   5
  64   6
 128   7

To set more than one bit, use a combination of the above
values. To check if a bit in a memory location is set, you
must POKE (LOC),PEEK(LOC) AND X, where again X comes from
the above table.

Basic keywords

[X] indicates the name of a parameter.

AUDIO

Connects or disconnects cassette output to TV, for recording sound effects on tape to be played back later using MOTOR command.

AUDIO ON
AUDIO OFF

CIRCLE

Draws a circle on the graphics screen.

CIRCLE ([X],[Y]),[R],[list of attributes]

X indicates X co-ordinate of position of centre of circle.
Y indicates Y co-ordinate of position of centre of circle.
R indicates radius of circle.

[list of attributes] is made up as follows.

[C],[HW],[START],[END]

C indicates colour of circle.
HW indicates the height/width ratio (for ellipses).
START indicates starting position of circle.
END indicates end position of circle.

CLEAR

Resets all variables to zero if numeric , or null strings if string, reserves space for strings, and sets top of BASIC.

CLEAR [string space],[address]

string space is the number of bytes reserved for strings.
address is the highest address that BASIC will use.

CLOAD

Loads BASIC program from tape in either ASCII or token form.

CLOAD
CLOAD ""
CLOAD "[filename]"

CLOADM

Loads machine code program from tape.

CLOADM
CLOADM ""
CLOADM "[filename]"
CLOADM "",[offset]
CLOADM "[filename]",[offset]

offset moves program up in memory from the original saved
address.

CLOSE

Closes any open files or devices.

CLOSE [device number]

If device number is not specified, all files currently open
are closed.

CLS

Clears the screen and sets the background colour.

CLS [colour]

COLOR

Sets the background and foreground colours on a graphics
page.

COLOR [foreground],[background]

Note American spelling of colour!

CONT

Continues a program after execution has been halted. It
won't work if any program changes are made before issuing
the command.

CONT

CSAVE

Saves a BASIC program onto tape.

CSAVE
CSAVE ""
CSAVE "[filename]"
CSAVE "",[A]
CSAVE "[filename]",[A]

The 'A' will save the program in ASCII format.

CSAVEM

Saves a machine code program onto tape.

CSAVEM "",[start],[end],[entry]
CSAVEM "[filename]",[start],[end],[entry]

start indicates first address to be saved.
end indicates last address to be saved.
entry indicates first address to be executed.

DATA

Stores data in program. Data can be either string or
numeric, and quotation marks are not needed for strings
unless you're using a comma within that string.

DATA [number],[string],["string"]

DEF FN

Defines a numeric function.

DEF FN[name]([var])=[expression]

The variable (VAR) used will only affect the expression, and
won't change any variable of the same name elsewhere in the
program.

DEFUSR

Defines a machine code routine.

DEFUSR[n]=[address]

DEL

Deletes program lines.

DEL [X-Y]

Deletes from and including line X up to and including line
Y.

DEL [X-] deletes from line X onwards.
DEL [-Y] deletes from start of program to line Y.
DEL [-] deletes the entire program.
DEL [X] deletes line X.

DIM

Dimensions a string or numeric array.

DIM [array]([size]),[array]([size])

This defines an array to hold (size) number of elements.
Arrays can be multi-dimensional (e.g. DIM A$(2,2,2,2)).

14

DRAW

Draws a line on a graphics page.

DRAW [list of parameters]

The list of parameters may contain any or all of the
following, where X and Y are horizontal and vertical
co-ordinates and Z is simply the number of positions to be
moved:

M : move draw position (MX,Y or offset by M+X,+Y)
U : move/draw position up (UY)
D : move/draw position down (UY)
L : move/draw position left (UX)
R : move/draw position right (UX)
E : move/draw position at 45 degree angle (EZ)
F : ditto but at 135 degrees (FZ)
G : ditto but at 225 degrees (GZ)
H : ditto but at 315 degrees (HZ)
X : execute a substring and return
C : change colour to whatever
A : tilt everything at an angle
S : scale everything
B : before any movement command ceases to draw but still
    moves
N : before any movement command doesn't update position
    but returns to original cursor position

Phew!

EDIT

Goes into edit mode.

EDIT [line]

In edit mode, there are a number of commands that can be
used:

xC : change x characters
xD : delete x characters
H   : delete rest of line and await new input
I   : insert new characters
K   : delete rest of line from current position
xKc : delete rest of line up to xth occurrence of
      character 'c'
L   : list current state of line
xSc : search through line for xth occurrence of
      character 'c'
X   : extend line and await new input

xSPACE   : move along x spaces
x([CL])   : move left x space (CL is left arrow
SHIFT([CU]) : leave insert mode and return to edit mode
ENTER   : leave edit mode and store line.

To recall a line as it was before you edited it, press
SHIFT([CU]), then press A and ENTER.

ELSE

See IF

END

Halts program execution.

END

EXEC

Transfers program execution to machine code routine.

EXEC [address]

Go to the address specified.

FOR

Start of a program loop.

FOR [variable]=[x1]TO[x2]STEP[x3] .... NEXT [variable]

Set the variable equal to x1. Increment it in steps of x3
(if omitted, this defaults to 1), and repeat it until the
variable is equal to x2 plus x3. Program execution is then
transferred to the statement immediately after the NEXT
statement.

If x1 is less than x2, then STEP must be used, and x3 must
be a negative number. The variable is then decremented on
each pass through the loop.

GET

This saves a rectangle of a graphics screen and stores it in
a variable array for later recall (see PUT).

GET ([X1],[Y1])-([X2],[Y2]),[variable],G

This saves the rectangle from the diagonally opposed corners
X1,Y1 and X2,Y2.   The G specifies 'save full graphic
detail'. It may be omitted.

GOSUB

This performs a subroutine.

GOSUB [line number]

This transfers program execution to [line number], where
execution continues until a RETURN statement is encountered.
When it is, the program returns to the statement following
the GOSUB.

GOTO

This transfers program execution to another line.

GOTO [line number]

IF
--

This indicates the start of a conditional relationship.

IF [condition] THEN [result] ELSE [another result]

If a condition is true, then we can either execute a
statement or branch to another line number. If it isn't,
program execution continues at the line after the IF
statement, unless the optional ELSE is used, in which case
the statement or line number specified after the ELSE is
executed.

INPUT

Used for getting data from the user via the keyboard.

INPUT "[prompt]";[variable1],[variable2],etc....

When this is used, program execution halts until the user
types something in and presses ENTER. If no prompt is
given, the semi-colon after it must be omitted.

INPUT#-1

Inputs data from tape.

INPUT#-1,[variable1],[variable2],etc....

This gets data from tape that has previously been saved
using PRINT#-1.

LET

This assigns a value to a variable.

LET [variable]=[expression]

The use of LET is optional.

LIST

This lists a program onto the screen. It is displayed at
great speed, and can be halted using the SHIFT and '@' keys
together.

LIST [X-Y]

This follows the same procedures for X and Y as DEL, except
that to list an entire program you must just enter LIST.

LLIST

This lists a program onto a line printer.

LLIST [X-Y]

This follows exactly the same procedures for X and Y as
LIST.

LINE

This, amazingly enough, draws a line!

LINE ([X1],[Y1]) - ([X2],[Y2]),[a],[b]

This draws a line from X1,Y1 to X2,Y2. If X1,Y1 is omitted,
the end point of the last LINE or DRAW is used as the
starting point. If there hasn't been a previous LINE or
DRAW, then X1,Y1 is assumed to be (126,96).

[a] is either PSET or PRESET. If PSET, then the line is
drawn in the foreground colour, if PRESET then the line is
drawn in the background colour and is thus effectively
erased.

[b] is either B or BF. If B, then a rectangle is drawn
using X1,Y1 and X2,Y2 as the two opposing corners.   If BF,
then a rectangle is still drawn, but it is also filled in
with the current foreground colour.

LINE INPUT

This allows data to be entered from the keyboard.

LINE INPUT "[prompt string]";[variable]
LINE INPUT [variable]

This works in the same way as INPUT, except that LINE INPUT
will take an entire line of input, including leading spaces,
blanks etc. Everything is then placed in a string variable.

Note that you cannot use numeric variables with LINE INPUT.

MOTOR

This turns the cassette motor on and off, allowing control
of the motor from within a program (see AUDIO).

MOTOR ON
MOTOR OFF

NEW

This removes the current BASIC program from memory.   It
doesn't actually wipe the memory out, but instead merely
changes a few internal pointers so that the program can no
longer be accessed.

See the 'Useful hints and tips' section for a method of
recovering a program that has accidentally been NEWed.

NEW

ON ... GOSUB

This is a multiple branching statement to a set of
subroutines.

ON [variable] GOSUB [line number1],[line number2], ...

If [variable] is equal to one, the program will branch to
the subroutine at [line number1], if it equals 2, it will
branch to [line number2], and so on. Be careful to match up
RETURNs with multiple GOSUB statements like this.

ON ... GOTO

As above, but this merely sends program execution to a
specified line, without expecting a RETURN to be found
there.

ON [variable] GOTO [line number1],[line number2], ...

OPEN

This opens a data file for reading or writing data.

OPEN "[a]",#-1,[filename]

If 'a' is set as 'O', then the file will be opened for
writing data, and if it's set to 'I' then the file will be
opened for reading data.

PAINT

This fills in a section of a graphics page.

PAINT ([X],[Y])
PAINT ([X],[Y]),[colour]

PAINT ([X],[Y]),[colour],[border]

This paints in a section of screen starting at the
co-ordinates X and Y, using the [colour] specified. If no
colour is named, then the foreground colour is assumed. It
fills in everything until it reaches a boundary coloured in
the [border] colour.

PCLEAR

This reserves memory for use with graphical displays.

PCLEAR [x]

This reserves 'x' graphics pages. If you're using text only
programs, use PCLEAR1 at the start of your program.

PCLS

This clears the current graphics page being used.

PCLS [x]

This clears the graphics page to colour [x]. If 'x' is not
specified, then the current background colour is used.

PCOPY

This copies graphics pages.

PCOPY [x] TO [y]

Copy graphics page x to graphics page y.

PLAY

Used for playing music, this is a multi-parameter command.

PLAY [command string]

where command string can contain any or all of the
following:

A-G   : musical notes
1-12   : musical tones
Ox   : octave x
Vx   : volume x
Lx   : length of note
Tx   : tempo
Px   : wait for x amount of time
Xx$: execute x string and return
or +   : sharp note
-        : flat note
.   : play note half as long again.

PMODE

This selects the resolution and graphics page to be used.

PMODE [x1],[x2]

This selects the resolution to be x1, and the graphics page
to be used to be x2. See the graphics section for further
information.

POKE

This puts a specific value into a specific memory location.

POKE [location],[value]

This puts the value [value] into memory location [location]

PRESET

This sets a specified X,Y co-ordinate on the graphics page
to the background colour.

PRESET ([X],[Y])

PRINT

This displays information on the screen.

PRINT "[expression]"[separator]"[expression"]etc....

If the expression is not within quotes, it can be either a
numeric or string variable.   Anything within quotes is
literally printed as it is written. The separator can be a
comma (splits output into two 15 column displays),   a
semi-colon (prints the next expression on the next column
space), or a space (as with a semi-colon, but the cursor
does not remain in its last print position).

PRINT USING

This is a very detailed way of formatting printed output.

PRINT USING [format string][output]

[output] is simply a list of variables to be printed,
separated by commas.

However, [format string] is a lot more daunting, and can
contain:

'.'   : indicates column to display decimal point in
'#'   : indicates column to display a digit
','   : put a comma to the left of every
             third digit before the decimal point
'**'   : fill all unfilled columns to the left with
             asterisks
'$'   : precede number with a dollar sign
'$$'   : place dollar sign immediately to left of number
             (i.e. not just at start of specified field)
'*$'   : fill unused columns to left of dollar sign with
             asterisks
'+'   : specify whether a number is positive or negative
             by displaying sign
'-'   : as above, but only specifies negative numbers
'[4CU]'   : display number in exponential form
'!'   : print only first character of a string
'%spc%'   : specifies the length (number of 'spc') to which
             a string variable will be printed

PRINT@

This prints the output at a specified location.

PRINT@ [location],[expression]

This prints the expression at the location numbered
(location lying between 0 and 511 on the screen).

PRINT#

Prints data to external devices.

PRINT#-1,[data]
PRINT#-2,[data]
PRINT USING#-1,[format string];[data]
PRINT USING#-2,[format string];[data]

This prints data either to cassette (#-1) or a printer
(#-2).

PSET

This sets a point on a graphics page to a specified colour.

PSET ([X],[Y],[C])

This sets the point X,Y to the colour C.

PUT

This puts a previously stored array (see GET) onto a
graphics page.

PUT ([X1],[Y1])-([X2],[Y2]),[a],[b]

This puts the array stored in [a] onto the graphics page at
top left hand corner X1,Y1 and bottom right hand corner
X2,Y2.

[b] determines how it is placed there. If [b] is PSET, then
all the points in the array are set. If it is PRESET, then
all the points are reset. If it is AND, then all points
common to the screen and the array are set, if it's OR, then
all points that are set on the screen OR in the array are
set, and if it's NOT, then that area of the screen is
reversed.

READ

This reads the next item from a DATA statement.

READ [variable1],[variable2], ...

See RESTORE.

REM

This allows remarks to be placed in a program, for greater
legibility when listing the program

REM [expression]
' [expression]

22

RENUM

Used for renumbering all or part of a program listing.

RENUM [newline],[startline],[increment]

This renumbers in steps of [increment], starting at the number [newline], commencing from the line [startline] in the old program. GOTOs, GOSUBs, IFs, THENs and ELSEs are all renumbered accordingly.

RESET

This sets a point on the text screen to the background colour.

RESET ([X],[Y])

In other words, the point at X,Y is effectively erased from the screen.

RESTORE

This allows previously READ data to be re-read.

RESTORE

The data pointer will now point back to the very first item of data.

RETURN

Returning from a subroutine.

RETURN

See GOSUB.

RUN

This commences program execution at either the first line, or a specified other line.

RUN [line number]

SCREEN

This sets a graphics or a text screen and the colour set to be used therein.

SCREEN [type],[colour set]

[type] is either 0 for text or 1 for graphics. [colour set] depends on current PMODE setting (see graphics commands and colour codes sections for further information).

SET

This sets a point on the text screen to a specified colour.
Any points other than the point specified in the character
block containing that point are re-set to black.

SET ([X],[Y],[C])

SKIPF

This allows you to move past a file on tape. If a filename
is specifed, the computer will run on through the tape until
the end of that file, and then stop the cassette motor.

SKIPF
SKIPF ""
SKIPF "[filename]"

SOUND

This generates a sound of a specified pitch and duration

SOUND [pitch],[duration]

STOP

From within a program, this terminates program execution.
The program can be re-started from the next executable
statement using CONT.

STOP

TRON and TROFF

This turns the trace mode on or off.

TRON
TROFF

Basic functions

ABS

This returns the absolute value of a number.

ABS ([number])

This will give us a numerical value, regardless of whether [number] is positive or negative.

ASC

This returns the Dragon's idea of the ASCII code for specified characters.

ASC ([string])

This gives us the ASCII code of the first character in [string].

ATN

This returns the arctangent of a number in radians. For those rusty on the geometry side, arctangent is the inverse of tangent.

ATN ([number])

As with all the geometric functions, numbers must be converted to radians before being used.

CHR$

This takes a number and prints out the ASCII character for that number. See the sections on ASCII characters for further information.

CHR$ ([number])

Some ASCII characters perform actions, as can be seen from the sections on ASCII characters.

COS

This returns the cosine of a number in radians.

COS ([number])

EOF

This indicates the end of a file from tape.

EOF ([file number])

More accurately, it tells us whether or not a given file
number has more data to come. If not, and a further INPUT
is specified, then an error occurs.

EXP

This is the inverse of LOG (see below).

EXP ([number]).

This raises the natural logarithm 'e' to the power [number].

FIX

A useful routine for removing all digits after the decimal
point of a number.

FIX ([number])

HEX$

This converts a number to hexadecimal.

HEX ([number])

This returns the hexadecimal string consisting of the digits
A to F and 0 to 9 which is represented by the decimal number
[number].

INKEY$

This is used for receiving one character at a time from the
keyboard.

INKEY$
Z$=INKEY$

Z$ will equal the last character pressed on the keyboard,
apart from those in INPUT etc. statements. In other words,
you may have INPUT something, and then issued an INKEY$
command. The INKEY$ command will sit and wait until
something is pressed.

INSTR

This searches a specified string for a specified sub-string.

INSTR ([number],[string1],[string2])

This searches through string1 for the occurrence of string2,
starting at the [number]th character of string1. This will

return either the starting position of string2, or a zero if
string2 is found not to exist in string1.

INT

This converts a number to integer format.

INT ([number])

This removes anything after the decimal point, and also
(which is were it differs from FIX), rounds numbers down
regardless of whether they are positive or negative.

JOYSTCK

This returns a value depending on the position of the
joystick (either left or right).

JOYSTCK ([number])

0 indicates the horizontal position of the right joystick.
2 indicates the horizontal position of the left joystick.
1 indicates the vertical position of the right joystick.
3 indicates the vertical position of the left joystick.

LEFT$

A string manipulation command that returns the LEFTmost
characters from a string.

LEFT$ ([string],[number])

This returns the leftmost [number] of characters from the
string [string].

LEN

This returns the LENgth of a specified string.

LEN ([string])

This returns the number of characters in the string
[string], regardless of whether they are control characters,
text characters, or whatever.

LOG

This returns the natural logarithm of a number, which must
be a positive one.

LOG ([number])

MEM

This returns the amount of free memory still available to
the programmer in BASIC.

MEM

This memory is available for programs and data, and does not include any set aside for screen and graphics pages.

MID$

Another string manipulation command, which returns a specified part of a specified string.

MID$([string],[number1],[number2])

This returns a substring of [string], starting at the [number1]th character, and taking [number2] characters. [number2] may be omitted, in which case the substring will consist of all the characters in [string] from the [number1]th onwards.

This command can also work in reverse, in that part of a string can be replaced with another substring. For example:

A$="HELLO THERE MY FINE FELLOW"
MID$(A$,16,4)="UGLY"
PRINTA$

The result would be:

HELLO THERE MY UGLY FELLOW

PEEK

This returns the contents of a specified memory location

PEEK ([address])

This returns whatever value happens to be stored in memory location [address] at the time.

POINT

This checks for the presence of a dot on a text screen.

POINT ([X],[Y])

If there is a text character at location X,Y then a -1 is returned, if there's nothing there a zero is returned, otherwise the current colour of the dot is returned.

POS

Unusual in that on the Dragon this works for both screen and printer, this returns the current horizontal position of the cursor.

POS ([number])

Here, if the number was equal to 0 the position returned would refer to the screen, and if it equalled 1 the position returned would refer to the printer.

PPOINT

Same as POINT, only this time we're checking for a dot on
the graphics screen.

PPOINT ([X],[Y])

If the location specified is turned off, a 0 is returned,
otherwise the colour of the dot is returned.

RIGHT$

Another string manipulation command, this returns the
RIGHTmost specified number of characters from within a
specified string.

RIGHT$ ([string],[number])

This returns the rightmost [number] characters from within
[string].

RND

This is used for generating integer random numbers.

RND ([number])

This returns an integer random number in the range 1 and
number. If RND is used without a number, then a real number
between 0 and 1 is returned.

To generate a number in the range X to Y, use the formula:

RND(X-1)+Y-X+1

SGN

This returns the sign (positive, negative or zero) of a
number.

SGN ([number])

-1 is returned if the number's negative, 0 if it equals
zero, and +1 if it is positive.

SIN

Another geometric function, this returns the sine of a
number, assuming that the number is expressed in radians.

SIN ([number])

STRING$

This is used for building up strings of specified length.

STRING$ ([number1],[number2])

STRING$ ([number1],[string])

In the first instance, a string will be made of length
[number1], consisting of the character whose code is
[number2]. In the second example, the string will again be
of length [number1], but will consist this time of the first
character contained in [string].

STR$

This performs a numeric to string conversion.

STR$([number])

This will convert the number contained within [number] into
a string, but note that it also adds a leading space to the
new string (unlike some machines, which add control
characters!).

SQR

This finds the square root of a number.

SQR ([number])

If [number] is negative, then the program will report an
error code.

TAN

Our final geometrical function, this returns the tangent of
a number, assuming that the number is expressed in radians.

TAN ([number])

TIMER

This either sets or returns the variable TIMER.

TIMER
TIMER= ([number])

In the first case, the computer will print out the length of
time, in fiftieths of a second, that it has been switched on
for. However, if the value stored in TIMER exceeds 65535,
then it is reset to zero.

In the second example, TIMER acts as a variable and is given
the value [number]. It will still be incremented every
fiftieth of a second (approximately).

USR

This calls a user-defined machine code routine that was
earlier defined using DEF USR.

USR [n]([number])

VAL

The opposite of STR$, this converts a string back to a
number again.

VAL ([string]).

This returns the numeric value of the string contained in
[string]. If [string] contains a non-numeric character,
then only characters to the left of that are considered.

VARPTR

This gives the memory location of where a variable is stored
in memory.

VARPTR ([number])

This returns the start address of where the variable in
[number] is stored. With arrays, if number was equal to,
say, the first element of the array A(15), then the value
returned would be the start location for that first element.
Other elements could then be found, since each one occupies
5 bytes of memory.

Basic error messages

The Dragon is not equipped with the best set of error messages on a home computer, as a glance below will show. How many people can remember what a DS error is? The table below contains them all, including the two Dragon forgot about.

These are only the error messages generated by the computer itself when NOT used with disk drives. There's an additional set of messages for those (some are repeated e.g. FD ERROR can mean Bad File Data, or Full Directory!), and they are repeated at the back of the disk drive manual, albeit in cryptic form. But, since this is for the computer, and since the computer manual doesn't list all of them anyway, here we go.

```
MESSAGE    EXPLANATION
-------    -----------
```

/O   An attempt has been made to divide by zero.

AO   An attempt has been made to open a file which
         is already open.

BS   This usually occurs when an attempt has been
         made to use an array subscript that is outside
         range it was defined to lie in.

CN   A 'can't continue error'. Usually when the user
         has typed in CONT after altering a program.

DD   A 're-dimensioned array error', when an attempt
         has been made to re-dimension an already
         dimensioned array.

DN (*)   A device number error, which refers either
         to the screen or keyboard, the tape deck, or the
         printer.

DS   A direct statement error, which usually occurs
         when a data file on tape contains a direct
         statement.

FC   An illegal function call error, which occurs when
         a parameter is out of range, either in a
         statement or a function.

FD   A 'file data' error. This occurs when the wrong
         type of data is being read in from a data file.
         That is, a string variable is trying to be read
         into a numeric one, or vice versa.

MESSAGE   EXPLANATION
-------   -----------

FM   A 'file mode' error. This happens when you try
          to input data to a file that is waiting for
          output, or attempt to output data to an input
          file.

ID   An illegal direct statement. This occurs when
          you've attempted to use in direct mode a command
          that can only be executed from within a program.

IE   An attempt has been made to input data from
          beyond the end of a file.

IO   An Input/Output error. This is either caused by
          incorrect adjustment of the cassette deck (e.g.
          volume too high or too low), or by a tape that
          is faulty.

LS   A 'string too long' error, which occurs when a
          string exceeds 255 characters in length.

NF   A 'next without for' error, which occurs when a
          NEXT statement is found where it wasn't expected
          (i.e. there is no corresponding FOR statement)

NO   A file hasn't been opened, and you can't read
          from or write to a file without opening it first.

OD   An 'out of data' error. An attempt has been made
          to read some data that doesn't exist, or there
          are no elements left to read in a data statement.

OM   An 'out of memory' error. This occurs when there
          is absolutely no memory left (either free or
          unreserved) in the computer.

OS   No room left for strings, since it's all been
          taken up. To correct, you can either try a
          CLEAR, or reserve more string space at the
          start of your programs.

OV   An overflow error. The result of a calculation
          is too large for the computer to handle.

RG   A 'return without gosub' error. That is, the
          computer has found a RETURN statement without
          a corresponding GOSUB statement.

SN   The most common one of all, a syntax error!
          This occurs when the Dragon can't understand
          something, usually as the result of a spelling
          mistake, a missing space or punctuation mark,
          or an incorrect number of parameters.

ST   A 'string formula too complex' error. That is,
          a string formula within a BASIC statement is
          too long, so you'll have to break it up a bit.

TM   A 'type mismatch' error, which occurs when numeric
          data is assigned to a variable, or vice versa.

MESSAGE   EXPLANATION
-------   -----------

UF (*)   An 'unidentified function' error, which occurs
           when an attempt has been made to use a function
           that has not previously been defined in the
           program.

UL   An 'unidentified line number' error, which occurs
           when the program attempts to branch to a line
           which doesn't exist.

(*)   Error code not in original manual.

34

Cassette port

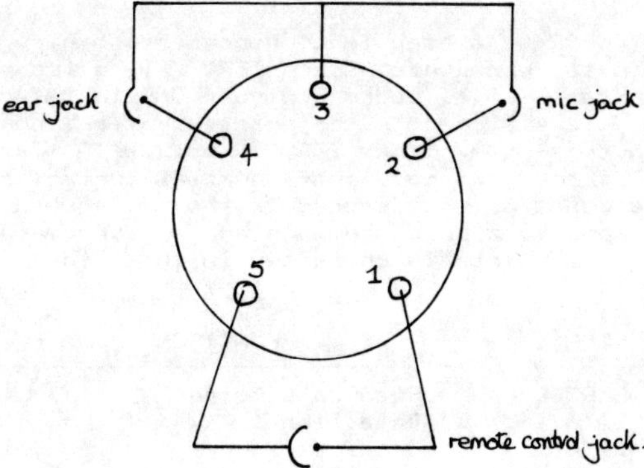

Centronics standards

<pre>
                        CENTRONICS PARALLEL INTERFACE

Notes

Busy is set if:

  1) Data is being received.
  2) Printer is printing.
  3) Printer is offline.
  4) An error condition is present.

On pins 02-09 a high level represents binary ONE, a
low level represents binary ZERO. All printable
characters (i.e. codes having a ONE in DATA 6 or
DATA 7) are stored in the printer buffer. Control
characters (i.e. codes ZERO in both DATA 6 and
DATA 7) are used to specify special control functions.
These codes are not stored in the buffer except when
they specify a print command and are preceded by at
least one printable character in that line.

PIN   CODE   FUNCTION
--------+-------------+-------------------------------------
  01   STROBE   Read Data Pulse.
  02   DATA 1   Data lines.
  03   DATA 2   ditto.
  04   DATA 3   ditto.
  05   DATA 4   ditto.
  06   DATA 5   ditto.
  07   DATA 6   ditto.
  08   DATA 7   ditto.
  09   DATA 8   ditto.
  10   ACKNLG   Data Received and Ready for More.
  11   BUSY   Not Ready for Data.
  12   PE   SET high when Out-of-Paper.
  13   +5V
  14   AUTO FEED   Switch Set gives extra line-feed.
  15   NC   No Connection.
  16   GND LOGIC   Logic Ground.
  17   GND CASE   Chassis Ground.
  18   NC   No Connection.
19-30   GND   Signal Grounds.
  31   INT   Reset and Buffer Clear.
  32   ERROR   See Notes on BUSY.
  33   GND   Signal Ground.
  34   NC   No Connection.
  35   +5V
  36   SLCT IN   Optional DC1/DC3.

</pre>

Character codes

HEX	DEC	Ø	1Ø	2Ø	3Ø	4Ø	5Ø	6Ø	7Ø
		Ø	16	32	48	64	80	96	112
Ø	Ø	@	P		Ø	@	P		Ø
1	1	A	Q	!	1	A	Q	!	1
2	2	B	R	"	2	B	R	"	2
3	3	C	S	#	3	C	S	#	3
4	4	D	T	$	4	D	T	$	4
5	5	E	U	%	5	E	U	%	5
6	6	F	V	8	6	F	V	8	6
7	7	G	W	'	7	G	W	'	7
8	8	H	X	(	B	H	X	(	8
9	9	I	Y	)	9	I	Y	)	9
A	10	J	Z	*	:	J	Z	*	:
B	11	K	[	+	;	K	[	+	;
C	12	L	÷	,	÷	L	÷	,	÷
D	13	M	]	—	=	M	]	—	=
E	14	N	÷	•	÷	N	÷	•	÷
F	15	O	—	/	?	O	—	/	?

HEX	DEC	2Ø	3Ø	4Ø	5Ø	6Ø	7Ø
	DEC	32	48	64	8Ø	96	112
Ø	Ø		Ø	@	P	@	P
1	1	!	1	A	Q	A	Q
2	2	"	2	B	R	B	R
3	3	#	3	C	S	C	S
4	4	$	4	D	T	D	T
5	5	%	5	E	U	E	U
6	6	&	6	F	V	F	V
7	7	'	7	G	W	G	W
8	8	(	8	H	X	H	X
9	9	)	9	I	Y	I	Y
A	1Ø	*	:	J	Z	J	Z
B	11	+	;	K	[	K	[
C	12	,	÷	L	÷	L	÷
D	13	—	=	M	]	M	]
E	14	•	÷	N	÷	N	÷
F	15	/	?	O	—	O	—

Colour codes

PMODE #	Colour Set	Two-Colour Combination	Four-Colour Combination
4	Ø	Black / Green	—
	1	Black / Buff	—
3	Ø	—	Green / Yellow / Blue / Red
	1	—	Buff / Cyan / Magenta / Orange
2	Ø	Black / Green	—
	1	Black / Buff	—
1	Ø	—	Green / Yellow / Blue / Red
	1	—	Buff / Cyan / Magenta / Orange
Ø	Ø	Black / Green	—
	1	Black / Buff	—

CODE	COLOUR
Ø	Black
1	Green
2	Yellow
3	Blue
4	Red
5	Buff
6	Cyan
7	Magenta
8	Orange

Disk commands

For the benefit of those with disk drives who'd like a handy
list of all the new commands, here we go:


```
Command        Purpose
-------        -------


AUTO           Generate automatic line numbers.
BACKUP         Makes a backup copy of a whole disk.
BEEPx          Makes x separate beeps.
BOOT           Boots a new operating system into RAM.
CHAIN          Loads and runs a BASIC program with all
               variables intact.
CLOSE          Closes all disk files.
COPY           Copies files from one disk to the same disk,
               or another one.
CREATE         Reserves disk space for a file.
DIR            Prints out the disk directory.
DRIVEx         Selects a drive (from 1 to 4).
DSK INIT       Formats a disk.
ERL            Gives the line at which the last error
               occurred.
ERR            Gives the code of the last error generated.
ERROR GOTOx    Jump to line x if an error occurs.
FLREAD         Reads a record from a file (like LINE INPUT).
FRE$           Gives the amount of free string space.
FREAD          Reads a record from a file.
FREE           Gives the number of free bytes on a disk.
FWRITE         Writes a record to a file.
HIMEM          Gives highest memory location used by BASIC.
KILL           Erases a file from disk.
LOAD           Used to load BASIC or machine code programs.
LOC            Gives position of the read pointer.
LOF            Gives the length of a file in bytes.
MERGE          Merges a file from disk.
PROTECT        Protects files against accidental erasure.
RENAME         Renames a file on disk.
RUN "name"     Loads and runs BASIC programs.
SAVE           Saves BASIC or machine code programs.
SREAD          Reads a record from a specific sector.
SWAP A.B       Swaps the values of A and B.
SWRITE         Writes a file to a specific sector.
VERIFY         Turns off and on automatic  verifying.
WAITx          Pauses program execution for x milliseconds.
```

Edge connector

This 40 pin connector is configured as follows:

```
PIN NUMBER          PURPOSE
----------          -------


1                   -12V

2                   +12V

3                   HALT

4                   NMI

5                   RESET

6                   E  (6809 CLOCK)

7                   Q  (6809 CLOCK)

8                   CB1

9                   +5V

10-17               D0-D7

18                  READ/WRITE

19-31               A0-A12

32                  C000-FEFF (CHIP SELECT)

33-34               0V

35                  ANALOGUE IN

36                  FF40-FF5F SELECT

37-39               A13-A15

40                  TURNS OFF INTERNAL ROM
```

Flow charting

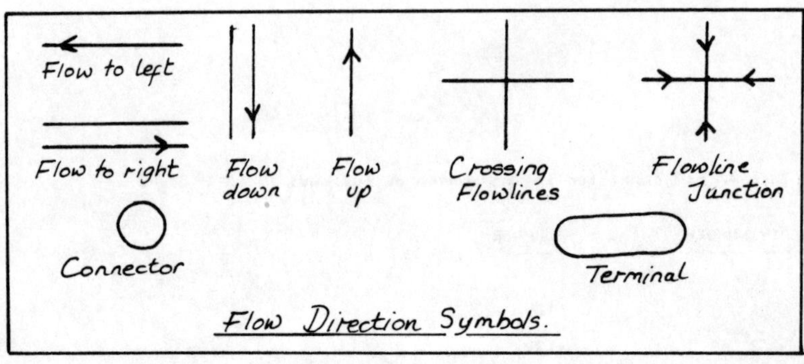

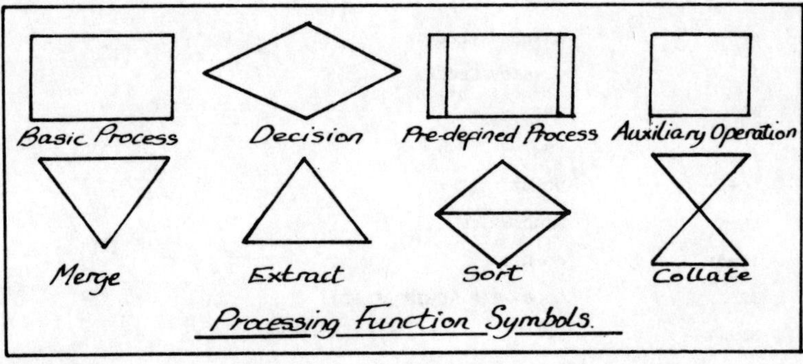

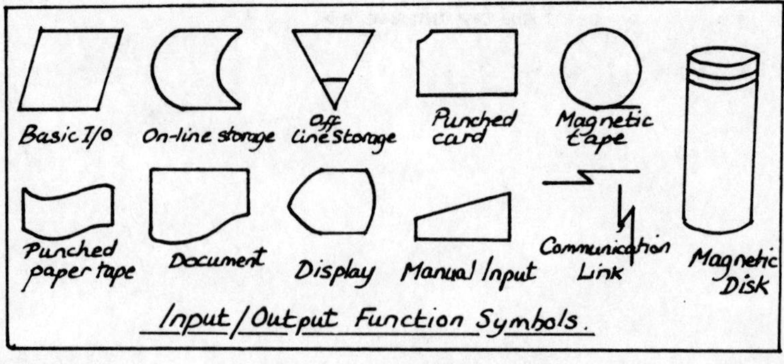

Graphics notes

The graphics capabilities of the Dragon are probably
superior to those of almost any other home computer, and yet
their use (and documentation) remain a mystery to most.

In this (and in the 'Useful Hints and Tips' section), we're
going to try to cram in as much graphical information as
possible. You've got the actual commands in the two earlier
sections on BASIC, so without further ado let's start on
graphics modes.

There are actually 14 of these, although only seven are
implemented on the Dragon's version of BASIC.

Mode	Resolution X	Resolution Y	Implemented in BASIC	Number of colours per screen	Number of bytes per screen
1 (A/N)	32	16	Yes	2	0.5K
2 (S/G 4)	64	32	Yes	8	0.5K
3 (S/G 6)	64	48	No	4	0.5K
4 (S/G 8)	64	64	No	8	2.0K
5 (S/G 12)	64	96	No	8	3.0K
6 (S/G 24)	64	192	No	8	6.0K
7 Graphic	64	64	No	4	1.0K
9 Graphic	128	64	No	2	1.0K
10 Graphic	128	96	Yes	2	1.5K
11 Graphic	128	96	Yes	4	3.0K
12 Graphic	128	192	Yes	2	3.0K
13 Graphic	128	192	Yes	4	6.0K
14 Graphic	256	192	Yes	2	6.0K

Note: A/N signifies alphanumeric.
      S/G signifies semigraphical.

Screens and pages

The video memory is divided up even further than this into
the text screen section and the graphics screen section,
which is itself divided up into 8 pages, each one taking up
1.5K of memory.

Decimal	Hex	Page	PMODE0	PMODE1&2	PMODE3&4
13824	3600				
		PAGE 8	PMODE0 SCREEN8		
12288	3000			PMODE1&2 SCREEN4	
		PAGE 7	PMODE0 SCREEN7		
10752	2A00				PMODE3&4 SCREEN2
		PAGE 6	PMODE0 SCREEN6		
9216	2400			PMODE1&2 SCREEN3	
		PAGE 5	PMODE0 SCREEN5		
7680	1E00				
		PAGE 4	PMODE0 SCREEN4		
6144	1800			PMODE1&2 SCREEN2	
		PAGE 3	PMODE0 SCREEN3		
4608	1200				PMODE3&4 SCREEN1
		PAGE 2	PMODE0 SCREEN2		
3072	0C00			PMODE1&2 SCREEN1	
		PAGE 1	PMODE0 SCREEN1		
1536	0600				
1024	0400	TEXT SCREEN	STANDARD TEXT AND SEMIGRAPHICS4		

Screen start addresses

There is a 7 bit register in the video graphics chip which determines where the start of the screen will be in memory. To get the actual memory location, the value in this register must be multiplied by 512. Being a 7 bit register, it is controlled by 14 (2 per bit) different memory locations, as indicated below.

BIT NUMBER	MEMORY LOCATION		ACTION
	HEX	DEC	
6	FFD3	65491	SET BIT 6
6	FFD2	65490	RESET BIT 6
5	FFD1	65489	SET BIT 5
5	FFD0	65488	RESET BIT 5
4	FFCF	65487	SET BIT 4
4	FFCE	65486	RESET BIT 4
3	FFCD	65485	SET BIT 3
3	FFCC	65484	RESET BIT 3
2	FFCB	65483	SET BIT 2
2	FFCA	65482	RESET BIT 2
1	FFC9	65481	SET BIT 1
1	FFC8	65480	RESET BIT 1
0	FFC7	65479	SET BIT 0
0	FFC6	65478	RESET BIT 0

PMODES

For different PMODEs and colour-sets, there are a variety of
different colours available to us. Needless to say, the
greater the resolution displayed on screen, the fewer
colours we have access to.

The following table shows the various relationships.

```
=================================================================
=PMODE No.  Colour set  Colours Available                       =
=================================================================
=                                                               =
=   4          0        Black/Green                             =
=   4          1        Black/Buff                              =
=   3          0        Green/Yellow/Blue/Red                   =
=   3          1        Buff/Cyan/Magenta/Orange               =
=   2          0        Black/Green                             =
=   2          1        Black/Buff                              =
=   1          0        Green/Yellow/Blue/Red                   =
=   1          1        Buff/Cyan/Magenta/Orange               =
=   0          0        Black/Green                             =
=   0          1        Black/Buff                              =
=================================================================
```

The next table shows how our selection of PMODE number
determines how many screens we can store in memory at the
same time, and therefore how many screens we can have access
to at once for producing animated effects.

```
=================================================================
= PMODE No.       Pages/Screen    No. of screens                =
=================================================================
=                                                               =
=   4                 4                 2                        =
=   3                 3                 2                        =
=   2                 2                 4                        =
=   1                 2                 4                        =
=   0                 1                 8                        =
=                                                               =
=================================================================
```

Description of graphics modes

As we've seen earlier in this graphics section, although the
Dragon only allows us to use 7 different graphics modes,
there are in fact 14 available altogether on the video chip
itself.

However, since you can only use 7 of them, there seems
little point in going into a detailed description of how all
of them work. Thus the following tables refer only to the 7
modes that we can access.

Each table will show the resolution available, the amount of
memory required to store a screen, and so on.

===

MODE1
=====

Type: Alphanumeric/Normal Text

Resolution: 32 by 16

Characters displayed: in normal format.

How they are stored in memory:

```
0        Line 1 Character 1
1        Line 1 Character 2
.            .
.            .
.            .
.            .
.            .
32       Line 2 Character 1
33       Line 2 Character 2
```

The numbers relate to the amount by which the start address
of the screen is offset to display that character.

Amount of memory required for screen: 0.5K

Memory address of any char. at (X,Y) = 32*Y+X+START ADDRESS

Border Colour: Black
Foreground colour: Colourset1=Orange
                   Colourset0=Green

How to select this screen:

This is the standard screen at power on.

===

===

MODE2
=====

Type: Semi Graphic 4

Resolution: 32 by 16

Characters displayed: in quarter squares.

How they are stored in memory:

```
    0       Line 1 Character 1
    1       Line 1 Character 2
    .             .
    .             .
    .             .
    .             .
    .             .
   32       Line 2 Character 1
   33       Line 2 Character 2
```

The numbers relate to the amount by which the start address
of the screen is offset to display that character.

Amount of memory required for screen: 0.5K

Memory address of any char. at (X,Y) = 32*Y+X+START ADDRESS

Border Colour: Black
Character Colour: Bits Set   Colour
                      000   Green
                      001   Yellow
                      010   Blue
                      011   Red
                      100   Buff
                      101   Cyan
                      110   Magenta
                      111   Orange

Bits set refers to bits 4,5 and 6 of each memory location on
the screen.

How to select this screen:

Set/Reset when in text mode.

===

==

MODE10
=====

Type: Graphics only

Resolution: 128 by 96 (two colours)

How they are stored in memory:

```
0       Row 1 Columns 1 to 8
1       Row 1 Columns 9 to 16
.               .
16      Row 2 Columns 1 to 8
.               .
.               .
.               .
1534    Row 96 Columns 113 to 120
1535    Row 96 Columns 121 to 128
```

The numbers relate to the amount by which the start address
of the screen is offset to display that character.

Amount of memory required for screen: 1.5K

Memory address of any char. at (X,Y) =
ROW*16+FIX((COLUMN-1)/8)+START ADDRESS

Border Colour: Green (colour set 0)
               Buff (colour set 1)
Character Colour: Bits Set Colour
                      0   Black (colour set 0)
                      1   Green (colour set 0)
                      0   Black (colour set 1)
                      1   Buff (colour set 0)

Bits set refers to individual bit for each pixel on screen.

How to select this screen:

PMODE0

==

===

MODE11
=====

Type: Graphic only (4 colours)

Resolution: 128 by 96

How characters are stored in memory:

As bit pairs, and thus each byte holds four columns.

Amount of memory required for screen: 3.0K

Memory address of any char. at (X,Y) =
32*ROW+FIX((COLUMN-1)/4)+START ADDRESS

Border Colour: Green (colour set 0)
               Buff (colour set 1)

Character Colour: Bits Set   Colour
                     00   Green   (colour set 0)
                     01   Yellow   (colour set 0)
                     10   Blue   (colour set 0)
                     11   Red   (colour set 0)
                     00   Buff   (colour set 1)
                     01   Cyan   (colour set 1)
                     10   Magenta (colour set 1)
                     11   Orange   (colour set 1)

Bits set refers to the bit pairs for each byte of on-screen
memory.

How to select this screen:

PMODE1

===

==

MODE12
=====

Type: Graphic only (2 colours)

Resolution: 128 by 192
How characters are stored in memory:

As individual bits, and thus each byte holds eight columns.

Amount of memory required for screen: 3.0K

Memory address of any char. at (X,Y) =
16*ROW+FIX((COLUMN-1)/8)+START ADDRESS

Border Colour: Green (colour set 0)
               Buff (colour set 1)

Character Colour: Bits Set Colour
                      1   Green   (colour set 0)
                      0   Black   (colour set 0)
                      1   Buff   (colour set 1)
                      0   Black   (colour set 1)

Bits set refers to the individual bit for each byte of
on-screen memory.

How to select this screen:

PMODE2

==

51

```
================================================================
```

MODE13
=====

Type: Graphic only (4 colours)

Resolution: 128 by 192
How characters are stored in memory:

As bit pairs, and thus each byte holds four columns.

Amount of memory required for screen: 6.0K

Memory address of any char. at (X,Y) =
32*ROW+FIX((COLUMN-1)/4)+START ADDRESS

Border Colour: Green (colour set 0)
               Buff (colour set 1)

Character Colour: Bits Set Colour
                      00   Green   (colour set 0)
                      01   Yellow   (colour set 0)
                      10   Blue   (colour set 0)
                      11   Red   (colour set 0)
                      00   Buff   (colour set 1)
                      01   Cyan   (colour set 1)
                      10   Magenta (colour set 1)
                      11   Orange   (colour set 1)

Bits set refers to the bit pairs for each byte of on-screen
memory.

How to select this screen:

PMODE3

```
================================================================
```

===

MODE14
=====

Type: Graphic only (2 colours)

Resolution: 256 by 192
How characters are stored in memory:

As individual bits, and thus each byte holds eight columns.

Amount of memory required for screen: 6.0K

Memory address of any char. at (X,Y) =
16*ROW+FIX((COLUMN-1)/8)+START ADDRESS

Border Colour: Green (colour set 0)
               Buff (colour set 1)

Character Colour: Bits Set Colour
                      1   Green   (colour set 0)
                      0   Black   (colour set 0)
                      1   Buff   (colour set 1)
                      0   Black   (colour set 1)

Bits set refers to the individual bit for each byte of
on-screen memory.

How to select this screen:

PMODE4

===

Hex/Dec convertor

Decimal & Hexadecimal Conversions

```
----------------------------------------------------------------------
                         HEXADECIMAL COLUMNS
----------------------------------------------------------------------
     6             5             4            3          2         1
----------------------------------------------------------------------
 HEX    DEC    HEX    DEC    HEX    DEC    HEX  DEC   HEX DEC   HEX DEC
----------------------------------------------------------------------
 0          0   0          0   0          0   0      0   0    0   0    0
 1  1,048,576   1     65,536   1      4,096   1    256   1   16   1    1
 2  2,097,152   2    131,072   2      8,192   2    512   2   32   2    2
 3  3,145,728   3    196,608   3     12,288   3    768   3   48   3    3
 4  4,194,304   4    262,144   4     16,384   4  1,024   4   64   4    4
 5  5,242,880   5    327,680   5     20,480   5  1,280   5   80   5    5
 6  6,291,456   6    393,216   6     24,576   6  1,536   6   96   6    6
 7  7,340,032   7    458,752   7     28,672   7  1,792   7  112   7    7
 8  8,388,608   8    524,288   8     32,768   8  2,048   8  128   8    8
 9  9,437,184   9    589,824   9     36,864   9  2,304   9  144   9    9
 A 10,485,760   A    655,360   A     40,960   A  2,560   A  160   A   10
 B 11,534,336   B    720,897   B     45,056   B  2,816   B  176   B   11
 C 12,582,912   C    786,432   C     49,152   C  3,072   C  192   C   12
 D 13,631,488   D    851,968   D     53,248   D  3,328   D  208   D   13
 E 14,680,064   E    917,504   E     57,344   E  3,584   E  224   E   14
 F 15,728,640   F    983,040   F     61,440   F  3,840   F  240   F   15
----------------------------------------------------------------------
```

Notes.

To convert from hexadecimal to decimal, first find the corresponding
column position for each hexadécimal digit. Make a note of the
decimal equivalents, then add the noted values together to obtain the
converted decimal value.

To convert from decimal to hexadecimal, find the largest decimal
value in the table that will fit into the number to be converted.
Next make a note of the hex equivalent and column position. Calculate
the decimal remainder, and repeat the process on this and any
subsequent remainders.

Hyperbolic functions

FUNCTION	BASIC EQUIVALENT
SECANT	SEC(X)=1/COS(X)
COSECANT	CSC(X)=1/SIN(X)
COTANGENT	COT(X)=1/TAN(X)
INVERSE SINE	ARCSIN(X)=ATN(X/SQR(−X*X+1))
INVERSE COSINE	ARCCOS(X)=−ATN(X/SQR (−X*X +1)) +π/2
INVERSE SECANT	ARCSEC(X)=ATN(X/SQR(X*X−1))
INVERSE COSECANT	ARCCSC(X)=ATN(X/SQR(X*X−1)) +(SGN(X)−1*π/2
INVERSE COTANGENT	ARCOT(X)=ATN(X)+π/2
HYPERBOLIC SINE	SINH(X)=(EXP(X)−EXP(−X))/2
HYPERBOLIC COSINE	COSH(X)=(EXP(X)+EXP(−X))/2
HYPERBOLIC TANGENT	TANH(X)=EXP(−X)/(EXP(x)+EXP (−X))*2+1
HYPERBOLIC SECANT	SECH(X)=2/(EXP(X)+EXP(−X))
HYPERBOLIC COSECANT	CSCH(X)=2/(EXP(X)−EXP(−X))
HYPERBOLIC COTANGENT	COTH(X)=EXP(−X)/(EXP(X) −EXP(−X))*2+1
INVERSE HYPERBOLIC SINE	ARCSINH(X)=LOG(X+SQR(X*X+1))
INVERSE HYPERBOLIC COSINE	ARCCOSH(X)=LOG(X+SQR(X*X−1))
INVERSE HYPERBOLIC TANGENT	ARCTANH(X)=LOG((1+X)/(1−X))/2
INVERSE HYPERBOLIC SECANT	ARCSECH(X)=LOG((SQR (−X*X+1)+1/X)
INVERSE HYPERBOLIC COSECANT	ARCCSCH(X)=LOG((SGN(X)*SQR (X*X+1/x)
INVERSE HYPERBOLIC COTAN- GENT	ARCCOTH(X)=LOG((X+1)/(x−1))/2

Joystick slot

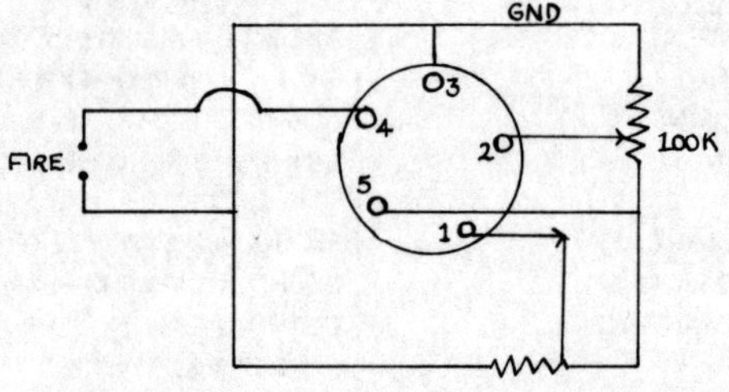

Low resolution grid

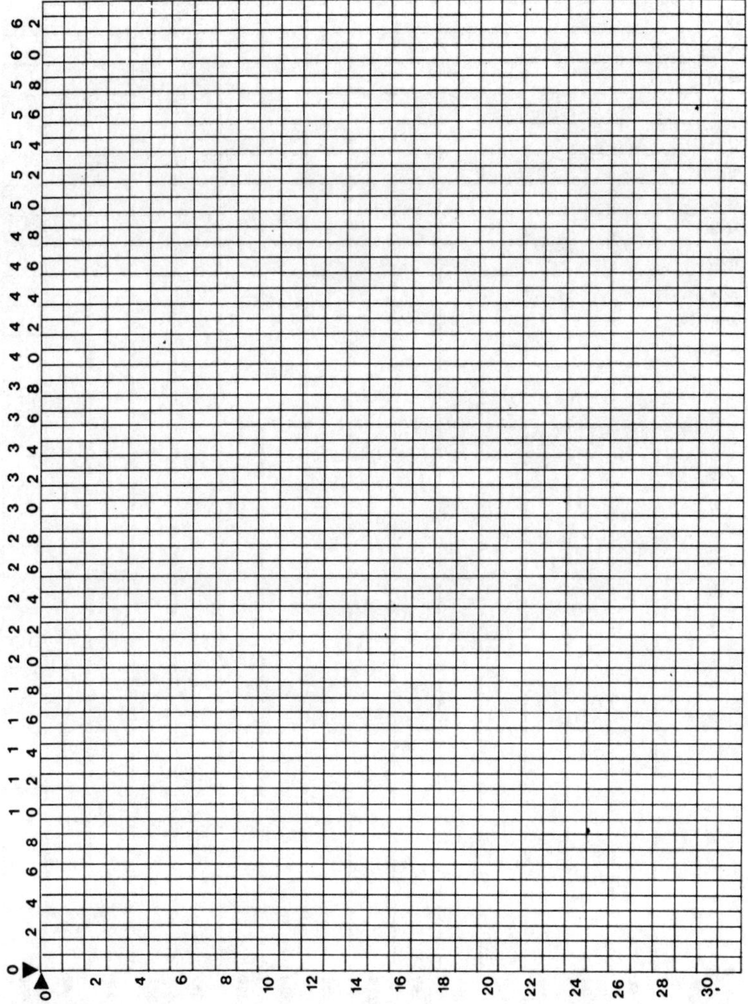

Print @ grid

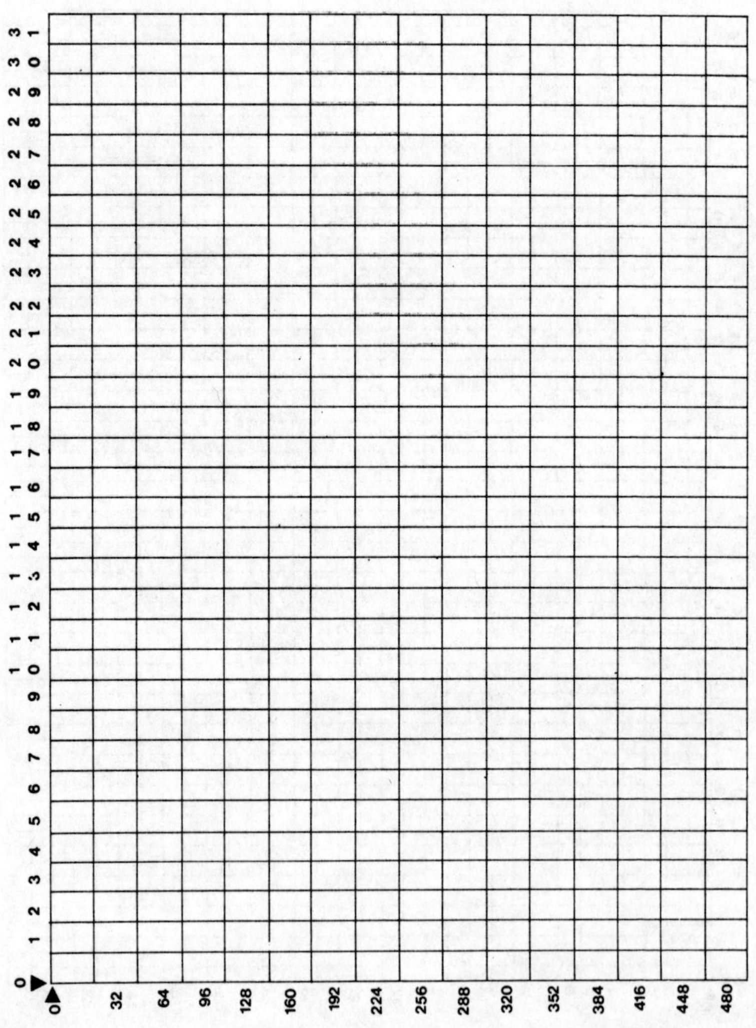

58

6809 M/C instruction set

INDEXED ADDRESSING MODES

TYPE	FORMS	NON INDIRECT				INDIRECT			
		Assembler Form	Post-Byte OP Code	+	+ #	Assembler Form	Post-Byte OP Code	+	+ #
CONSTANT OFFSET FROM R	NO OFFSET	, R	1RR00100	0	0	[, R]	1RR10100	3	0
	5 BIT OFFSET	n, R	0RRnnnnn	1	0	defaults to 8-bit			
	8 BIT OFFSET	n, R	1RR01000	1	1	[n, R]	1RR11000	4	1
	16 BIT OFFSET	n, R	1RR01001	4	2	[n, R]	1RR11001	7	2
ACCUMULATOR OFFSET FROM R	A—REGISTER OFFSET	A, R	1RR00110	1	0	[A, R]	1RR10110	4	0
	B—REGISTER OFFSET	B, R	1RR00101	1	0	[B, R]	1RR10101	4	0
	D—REGISTER OFFSET	D, R	1RR01011	4	0	[D, R]	1RR11011	7	0
AUTO INCREMENT/DECREMENT R	INCREMENT BY 1	, R+	1RR00000	2	0	not allowed			
	INCREMENT BY 2	, R++	1RR00001	3	0	[, R++]	1RR10001	6	0
	DECREMENT BY 1	, −R	1RR00010	2	0	not allowed			
	DECREMENT BY 2	, −−R	1RR00011	3	0	[, −−R]	1RR10011	6	0
CONSTANT OFFSET FROM PC	8 BIT OFFSET	n, PCR	1XX01100	1	1	[n, PCR]	1XX11100	4	1
	16 BIT OFFSET	n, PCR	1XX01101	5	2	[n, PCR]	1XX11101	8	2
EXTENDED INDIRECT	16 BIT ADDRESS	—	—	-	-	[n]	10011111	5	2

R = X, Y, U, or S
X = DON'T CARE

NOTES:

1 Given in the table are the base cycles and byte counts To determine the total cycles and byte counts add the values from the '6809 indexing modes' table.

2. R1 and R2 may be any pair of 8 bit or any pair of 16 bit registers
The 8 bit registers are A, B, CC, DP
The 16 bit registers are X, Y, U, S, D, PC

3 EA is the effective address.

4 The PSH and PUL instructions require 5 cycles plus 1 cycle for each *byte* pushed or pulled

5 5(6) means 5 cycles if branch not taken, 6 cycles if taken.

6 SW1 sets I&F bits SW12 and SW13 do not affect I&F

7 Conditions Codes set as a direct result of the instruction

8 Value of half-carry flag is undefined

9 Special Case—Carry set if b7 is SET

LEGEND:

OP	Operation Code (Hexadecimal);	Z	Zero (byte)
	Number of MPU Cycles;	V	Overflow, 2's complement
#	Number of Program Bytes.	C	Carry from bit 7
+	Arithmetic Plus;	‡	Test and set if true, cleared otherwise
-	Arithmetic Minus.	•	Not Affected
•	Multiply	CC	Condition Code Register
$\overline{M}$	Complement of M.	:	Concatenation
→	Transfer Into.	∨	Logical or
H	Half-carry from bit 3;	∧	Logical and
N	Negative (sign bit)	⊻	Logical Exclusive or

INSTRUCTION / FORMS		INHERENT			DIRECT			EXTENDED			IMMEDIATE			INDEXED[1]			RELATIVE			DESCRIPTION	5 H	3 N	2 Z	1 V	0 C
		OP	~	#	OP	~	#	OP	~	#	OP	~	#	OP	~	#	OP	~5	#						
ABX		3A	3	1																$B + X \to X$ (UNSIGNED)	•	•	•	•	•
ADC	ADCA				99	4	2	B9	5	3	89	2	2	A9	4+	2+				$A + M + C \to A$	↕	↕	↕	↕	↕
	ADCB				D9	4	2	F9	5	3	C9	2	2	E9	4+	2+				$B + M + C \to B$	↕	↕	↕	↕	↕
ADD	ADDA				9B	4	2	BB	5	3	8B	2	2	AB	4+	2+				$A + M \to A$	↕	↕	↕	↕	↕
	ADDB				DB	4	2	FB	5	3	CB	2	2	EB	4+	2+				$B + M \to B$	↕	↕	↕	↕	↕
	ADDD				D3	6	2	F3	7	3	C3	4	3	E3	6+	2+				$D + M{:}M + 1 \to D$	↕	↕	↕	↕	↕
AND	ANDA				94	4	2	B4	5	3	84	2	2	A4	4+	2+				$A \wedge M \to A$	•	↕	↕	0	•
	ANDB				D4	4	2	F4	5	3	C4	2	2	E4	4+	2+				$B \wedge M \to B$	•	↕	↕	0	•
	ANDCC										1C	3	2							$CC \wedge IMM \to CC$					1
ASL	ASLA	48	2	1																(shift left)	8	↕	↕	↕	↕
	ASLB	58	2	1																(shift left)	8	↕	↕	↕	↕
	ASL				08	6	2	78	7	3				68	6+	2+				(shift left)	8	↕	↕	↕	↕
ASR	ASRA	47	2	1																(shift right)	8	↕	↕	•	↕
	ASR	57	2	1																(shift right)	8	↕	↕	•	↕
	ASR				07	6	2	77	7	3				67	6+	2+				(shift right)	8	↕	↕	•	↕
BCC	BCC																24	3	2	Branch C = 0	•	•	•	•	•
	LBCC																10	5(6)	4	Long Branch C = 0	•	•	•	•	•
																	24								
BCS	BCS																25	3	2	Branch C = 1	•	•	•	•	•
	LBCS																10	5(6)	4	Long Branch C = 1	•	•	•	•	•
																	25								
BEQ	BEQ																27	3	2	Branch Z = 0	•	•	•	•	•
	LBEQ																10	5(6)	4	Long Branch Z = 0	•	•	•	•	•
																	27								
BGE	BGE																2C	3	2	Branch ≥ Zero	•	•	•	•	•
	LBGE																10	5(6)	4	Long Branch ≥ Zero	•	•	•	•	•
																	2C								
BGT	BGT																2E	3	2	Branch > Zero	•	•	•	•	•
	LBGT																10	5(6)	4	Long Branch > Zero	•	•	•	•	•
																	2E								
BHI	BHI																22	3	2	Branch Higher	•	•	•	•	•
	LBHI																10	5(6)	4	Long Branch Higher	•	•	•	•	•
																	22								
BHS	BHS																24	3	2	Branch Higher or Same	•	•	•	•	•
	LBHS																10	5(6)	4	Long Branch Higher or Same	•	•	•	•	•
																	24								
BIT	BITA				95	4	2	B5	5	3	85	2	2	A5	4+	2+				Bit Test A $(M \wedge A)$	•	↕	↕	0	•
	BITB				D5	4	2	F5	5	3	C5	2	2	E5	4+	2+				Bit Test B $(M \wedge B)$	•	↕	↕	0	•
BLE	BLE																2F	3	2	Branch ≤ Zero	•	•	•	•	•
	LBLE																10	5(6)	4	Long Branch ≤ Zero	•	•	•	•	•
																	2F								
BLO	BLO																25	3	2	Branch Lower	•	•	•	•	•
	LBLO																10	5(6)	4	Long Branch Lower	•	•	•	•	•
																	25								
BLS	BLS																23	3	2	Branch Lower or Same	•	•	•	•	•
	LBLS																10	5(6)	4	Long Branch Lower or Same	•	•	•	•	•
																	23								
BLT	BLT																2D	3	2	Branch < Zero	•	•	•	•	•
	LBLT																10	5(6)	4	Long Branch < Zero	•	•	•	•	•
																	2D								
BMI	BMI																2B	3	2	Branch Minus	•	•	•	•	•
	LBMI																10	5(6)	4	Long Branch Minus	•	•	•	•	•
																	2B								
BNE	BNE																26	3	2	Branch Z ≠ 0	•	•	•	•	•
	LBNE																10	5(6)	4	Long Branch Z ≠ 0	•	•	•	•	•
																	26								
BPL	BPL																2A	3	2	Branch Plus	•	•	•	•	•
	LBPL																10	5(6)	4	Long Branch Plus	•	•	•	•	•
																	2A								

INSTRUCTION	FORMS	INHERENT OP	~	#	DIRECT OP	~	#	EXTENDED OP	~	#	IMMEDIATE OP	~	#	INDEXED' OP	~	#	RELATIVE OP	~⁵	#	DESCRIPTION	H	N	Z	V	C
BRA	BRA																20	3	2	Branch Always	•	•	•	•	•
	LBRA																16	5	3	Long Branch Always	•	•	•	•	•
BRN	BRN																21	3	2	Branch Never	•	•	•	•	•
	LBRN																10 21	5	4	Long Branch Never	•	•	•	•	•
BSR	BSR																8D	7	2	Branch to Subroutine	•	•	•	•	•
	LBSR																17	9	3	Long Branch to Subroutine	•	•	•	•	•
BVC	BVC																28	3	2	Branch V = 0	•	•	•	•	•
	LBVC																10 28	5(6)	4	Long Branch V = 0	•	•	•	•	•
BVS	BVS																29	3	2	Branch V = 1	•	•	•	•	•
	LBVS																10 29	5(6)	4	Long Branch V = 1	•	•	•	•	•
CLR	CLRA	4F	2	1																$0 \to A$	•	0	1	0	0
	CLRB	5F	2	1																$0 \to B$	•	0	1	0	0
	CLR				0F	6	2	7F	7	3				6F	6+	2+				$0 \to M$	•	0	1	0	0
CMP	CMPA				91	4	2	B1	5	3	81	2	2	A1	4+	2+				Compare M from A	8	↕	↕	↕	↕
	CMPB				D1	4	2	F1	5	3	C1	2	2	E1	4+	2+				Compare M from B	8	↕	↕	↕	↕
	CMPD				10 93	7	3	10 B3	8	4	10 83	5	4	10 A3	7+	3+				Compare M: M + 1 from D	•	↕	↕	↕	↕
	CMPS				11 9C	7	3	11 BC	8	4	11 8C	5	4	11 AC	7+	3+				Compare M: M + 1 from S	•	↕	↕	↕	↕
	CMPU				11 93	7	3	11 B3	8	4	11 83	5	4	11 A3	7+	3+				Compare M: M + 1 from U	•	↕	↕	↕	↕
	CMPX				9C	6	2	BC	7	3	8C	4	3	AC	6+	2+				Compare M: M + 1 from X	•	↕	↕	↕	↕
	CMPY				10 9C	7	3	10 BC	8	4	10 8C	5	4	10 AC	7+	3+				Compare M: M + 1 from Y	•	↕	↕	↕	↕
COM	COMA	43	2	1																$\overline{A} \to A$	•	↕	↕	0	1
	COMB	53	2	1																$\overline{B} \to B$	•	↕	↕	0	1
	COM				03	6	2	73	7	3				63	6+	2+				$\overline{M} \to M$	•	↕	↕	0	1
CWAI		3C	20	2																CC ∧ IMM →CC: Wait for Interrupt					1
DAA		19	2	1																Decimal Adjust A	•	↕	↕	0	↕
DEC	DECA	4A	2	1																$A - 1 \to A$	•	↕	↕	↕	•
	DECB	5A	2	1																$B - 1 \to B$	•	↕	↕	↕	•
	DEC				0A	6	2	7A	7	3				6A	6+	2+				$M - 1 \to M$	•	↕	↕	↕	•
EOR	EORA				98	4	2	B8	5	3	88	2	2	A8	4+	2+				$A \veebar M \to A$	•	↕	↕	0	•
	EORB				D8	4	2	F8	5	3	C8	2	2	E8	4+	2+				$B \veebar M \to B$	•	↕	↕	0	•
EXG	R1, R2	1E	7	2																$R1 \leftrightarrow R2$[2]	•	•	•	•	•
INC	INCA	4C	2	1																$A + 1 \to A$	•	↕	↕	↕	•
	INCB	5C	2	1																$B + 1 \to B$	•	↕	↕	↕	•
	INC				0C	6	2	7C	7	3				6C	6+	2+				$M + 1 \to M$	•	↕	↕	↕	•
JMP					0E	3	2	7E	4	3				6E	3+	2+				$EA^3 \to PC$	•	•	•	•	•
JSR					9D	7	2	BD	8	3				AD	7+	2+				Jump to Subroutine	•	•	•	•	•
LD	LDA				96	4	2	B6	5	3	86	2	2	A6	4+	2+				$M \to A$	•	↕	↕	0	•
	LDB				D6	4	2	F6	5	3	C6	2	2	E6	4+	2+				$M \to B$	•	↕	↕	0	•
	LDD				DC	5	2	FC	6	3	CC	3	3	EC	5+	2+				$M:M + 1 \to D$	•	↕	↕	0	•
	LDS				10 DE	6	3	10 FE	7	4	10 CE	4	4	10 EE	6+	3+				$M:M + 1 \to S$	•	↕	↕	0	•
	LDU				DE	5	2	FE	6	3	CE	3	3	EE	5+	2+				$M:M + 1 \to U$	•	↕	↕	0	•
	LDX				9E	5	2	BE	6	3	8E	3	3	AE	5+	2+				$M:M + 1 \to X$	•	↕	↕	0	•
	LDY				10 9E	6	3	10 BE	7	4	10 8E	4	4	10 AE	6+	3+				$M:M + 1 \to Y$	•	↕	↕	0	•
LEA	LEAS													32	4+	2+				$EA^3 \to S$	•	•	•	•	•
	LEAU													33	4+	2+				$EA^3 \to U$	•	•	•	•	•
	LEAX													30	4+	2+				$EA^3 \to X$	•	•	↕	•	•
	LEAY													31	4+	2+				$EA^3 \to Y$	•	•	↕	•	•

INSTRUCTION	FORMS	INHERENT OP	~	#	DIRECT OP	~	#	EXTENDED OP	~	#	IMMEDIATE OP	~	#	INDEXED[1] OP	~	#	RELATIVE OP	~	#	DESCRIPTION	5 H	3 N	2 Z	1 V	0 C
LSL	LSLA	48	2	1																A } C ← b7...b0 ← 0	•	↕	↕	↕	↕
	LSLB	58	2	1																B }	•	↕	↕	↕	↕
	LSL				08	6	2	78	7	3				68	6+	2+				M } c b7 b0	•	↕	↕	↕	↕
LSR	LSRA	44	2	1																A } 0 → b7...b0 → C	•	0	↕	•	↕
	LSRB	54	2	1																B }	•	0	↕	•	↕
	LSR				04	6	2	74	7	3				64	6+	2+				M } b7 b0 c	•	0	↕	•	↕
MUL		3D	11	1																A × B → D (Unsigned)	•	•	↕	•	9
NEG	NEGA	40	2	1																$\overline{A}$ + 1 → A	8	↕	↕	↕	↕
	NEGB	50	2	1																$\overline{B}$ + 1 → B	8	↕	↕	↕	↕
	NEG				00	6	2	70	7	3				60	6+	2+				$\overline{M}$ + 1 → M	8	↕	↕	↕	↕
NOP		12	2	1																No Operation	•	•	•	•	•
OR	ORA				9A	4	2	BA	5	3	8A	2	2	AA	4+	2+				A ∨ M → A	•	↕	↕	0	•
	ORB				DA	4	2	FA	5	3	CA	2	2	EA	4+	2+				B ∨ M → B	•	↕	↕	0	•
	ORCC										1A	3	2							CC ∨ IMM → CC					7
PSH	PSHS	34	5+	2																Push Registers on S Stack	•	•	•	•	•
	PSHU	36	5+	2																Push Registers on U Stack	•	•	•	•	•
PUL	PULS	35	5+	2																Pull Registers from S Stack	•	•	•	•	•
	PULU	37	5+	2																Pull Registers from U Stack	•	•	•	•	•
ROL	ROLA	49	2	1																A }	•	↕	↕	↕	↕
	ROLB	59	2	1																B }	•	↕	↕	↕	↕
	ROL				09	6	2	79	7	3				69	6+	2+				M } c b7 ← b0	•	↕	↕	↕	↕
ROR	RORA	46	2	1																A }	•	↕	↕	•	↕
	RORB	56	2	1																B }	•	↕	↕	•	↕
	ROR				06	6	2	76	7	3				66	6+	2+				M } c b7 → b0	•	↕	↕	•	↕
RTI		3B	6/15	1																Return From Interrupt					7
RTS		39	5	1																Return From Subroutine	•	•	•	•	•
SBC	SBCA				92	4	2	B2	5	3	82	2	2	A2	4+	2+				A − M − C → A	8	↕	↕	↕	↕
	SBCB				D2	4	2	F2	5	3	C2	2	2	E2	4+	2+				B − M − C → B	8	↕	↕	↕	↕
SEX		1D	2	1																Sign Extend B into A	•	↕	↕	0	•
ST	STA				97	4	2	B7	5	3				A7	4+	2+				A → M	•	↕	↕	0	•
	STB				D7	4	2	F7	5	3				E7	4+	2+				B → M	•	↕	↕	0	•
	STD				DD	5	2	FD	6	3				ED	5+	2+				D → M: M + 1	•	↕	↕	0	•
	STS				10 DF	6	3	10 FF	7	4				10 EF	6+	3+				S → M: M + 1	•	↕	↕	0	•
	STU				DF	5	2	FF	6	3				EF	5+	2+				U → M: M + 1	•	↕	↕	0	•
	STX				9F	5	2	BF	6	3				AF	5+	2+				X → M: M + 1	•	↕	↕	0	•
	STY				10 9F	6	3	10 BF	7	4				10 AF	6+	3+				Y → M: M + 1	•	↕	↕	0	•
SUB	SUBA				90	4	2	B0	5	3	80	2	2	A0	4+	2+				A − M → A	8	↕	↕	↕	↕
	SUBB				D0	4	2	F0	5	3	C0	2	2	E0	4+	2+				B − M → B	8	↕	↕	↕	↕
	SUBD				93	6	2	B3	7	3	83	4	3	A3	6+	2+				D − M: M + 1 → D	•	↕	↕	↕	↕
SWI	SWI[a]	3F	19	1																Software Interrupt 1	•	•	•	•	•
	SWI2[a]	10 3F	20	2																Software Interrupt 2	•	•	•	•	•
	SWI3[a]	11 3F	20	2																Software Interrupt 3	•	•	•	•	•
SYNC		13	≥2	1																Synchronize to Interrupt	•	•	•	•	•
TFR	R1, R2	1F	7	2																R1 → R2[2]	•	•	•	•	•
TST	TSTA	4D	2	1																Test A	•	↕	↕	0	•
	TSTB	5D	2	1																Test B	•	↕	↕	0	•
	TST				0D	6	2	7D	7	3				6D	6+	2+				Test M	•	↕	↕	0	•

62

6809 mnemonics

OP	MNEM	MODE	~	#
ØØ	NEG	DIRECT	6	2
Ø3	COM	"	6	2
Ø4	LSR	"	6	2
Ø6	ROR	"	6	2
Ø7	ASR	"	6	2
Ø8	ASL/LSL	"	6	2
Ø9	ROL	"	6	2
ØA	DEC	"	6	2
ØC	INC	"	6	2
ØD	TST	"	6	2
ØE	JMP	"	3	2
ØF	CLR	DIRECT	6	2
12	NOP	INHERENT	2	1
13	SYNC	INHERENT	2	1
16	LBRA	RELATIVE	5	3
17	LBSR	RELATIVE	9	3
19	DAA	INHERENT	2	1
1A	ORCC	INMED	3	2

OP	MNEM	MODE	~	#
1C	ANDCC	INMED	3	2
1D	SEX	INHERENT	2	1
1E	EXG	"	8	2
1F	TFR	INHERENT	7	2
2Ø	BRA	RELATIVE	3	2
21	BRN	"	3	2
22	BHI	"	3	2
23	BLS	"	3	2
24	BHS/BCC	"	3	2
25	BLO/BCS	"	3	2
26	BNE	"	3	2
27	BEQ	"	3	2
28	BVC	"	3	2
29	BVS	"	3	2
2A	BPL	"	3	2
2B	BMI	"	3	2
2C	BGE	"	3	2
2D	BLT	RELATIVE	3	2

OP	MNEM	MODE	~	#
2E	BGT	RELATIVE	3	2
2F	BLE	"	3	2
3Ø	LEAX	INDEXED	4	2
31	LEAY	"	4	2
32	LEAS	"	4	2
33	LEAU	"	4	2
34	PSHS	INHERENT	5	2
35	PULS	"	5	2
36	PSHU	"	5	2
37	PULU	"	5	2
39	RTS	"	5	1
3A	ABX	"	3	1
3B	RTI	"	6/15	1
3C	CWAI	"	21	2
3D	MUL	"	11	1
3F	SWI	"	19	1
4Ø	NEGA	"	2	1
43	COMA	"	2	1

OP	MNEM	MODE	~	#
44	LSRA	INHERENT	2	1
46	RORA	"	2	1
47	ASRA	"	2	1
48	ASLA/LSLA	"	2	1
49	ROLA	"	2	1
4A	DECA	"	2	1
4C	INCA	"	2	1
4D	TSTA	"	2	1
4F	CLRA	"	2	1
5Ø	NEGB	"	2	1
53	COMB	"	2	1
54	LSRB	"	2	1
56	RORB	"	2	1
57	ASRA	"	2	1
58	ASLB/LSLB	"	2	1
59	ROLB	"	2	1
5A	DECB	"	2	1
5C	INCB	"	2	1

OP	MNEM	MODE	~	#
5D	TSTB	INHERENT	2	1
5F	CLRB	"	2	1
60	NEG	INDEXED	6	2
63	COM	"	6	2
64	LSR	"	6	2
66	ROR	"	6	2
67	ASR	"	6	2
68	ASL/LSL	"	6	2
69	ROL	"	6	2
6A	DEC	"	6	2
6C	INC	"	6	2
6D	TST	"	6	2
6E	JMP	"	3	2
6F	CLR	"	6	2
70	NEG	EXTENDED	7	3
73	COM	"	7	3
74	LSR	"	7	3
76	ROR	"	7	3

OP	MNEM	MODE	~	#
77	ASR	EXTENDED	7	3
78	ASL/LSL	"	7	3
79	ROL	"	7	3
7A	DEC	"	7	3
7C	INC	"	7	3
7D	TST	"	7	3
7E	JMP	"	4	3
7F	CLR	"	7	3
80	SUBA	IMMED	2	2
81	CMPA	"	2	2
82	SBCA	"	2	2
83	SUBD	"	4	3
84	ANDA	"	2	2
85	BITA	"	2	2
86	LDA	"	2	2
88	EORA	"	2	2
89	ADCA	"	2	2
8A	ORA	"	2	2

OP	MNEM	MODE	~	#
8B	ADDA	IMMED	2	2
8C	CMPX	"	4	3
8D	BSR	RELATIVE	7	2
8E	LDX	IMMED	3	3
90	SUBA	DIRECT	4	2
91	CMPA	"	4	2
92	SBCA	"	4	2
93	SUBD	"	6	2
94	ANDA	"	4	2
95	BITA	"	4	2
96	LDA	"	4	2
97	STA	"	4	2
98	EORA	"	4	2
99	ADCA	"	4	2
9A	ORA	"	4	2
9B	ADDA	"	4	2
9C	CMPX	"	6	2
9D	JSR	"	7	2

OP	MNEM	MODE	~	#
9E	LDX	DIRECT	5	2
9F	STX	"	5	2
A0	SUBA	INDEXED	4	2
A1	CMPA	"	4	2
A2	SBCA	"	4	2
A3	SUBD	"	6	2
A4	ANDA	"	4	2
A5	BITA	"	4	2
A6	LDA	"	4	2
A7	STA	"	4	2
A8	EORA	"	4	2
A9	ADCA	"	4	2
AA	ORA	"	4	2
AB	ADDA	"	4	2
AC	CMPX	"	6	2
AD	JSR	"	7	2
AE	LDX	"	5	2
AF	STX	"	5	2

OP	MNEM	MODE	~	#
BØ	SUBA	EXTENDED	5	3
B1	CMPA	"	5	3
B2	SBCA	"	5	3
B3	SUBD	"	7	3
B4	ANDA	"	5	3
B5	BITA	"	5	3
B6	LDA	"	5	3
B7	STA	"	5	3
B8	EORA	"	5	3
B9	ADCA	"	5	3
BA	ORA	"	5	3
BB	ADDA	"	5	3
BC	CMPX	"	7	3
BD	JSR	"	8	3
BE	LDX	"	6	3
BF	STX	"	6	3
CØ	SUBB	IMMED	2	2
C1	CMPB	"	2	2

OP	MNEM	MODE	~	#
C2	SBCB	IMMED.	2	2
C3	ADDD	"	4	3
C4	ANDB	"	2	2
C5	BITB	"	2	2
C6	LDB	"	2	2
C8	EORB	"	2	2
C9	ADCB	"	2	2
CA	ORB	"	2	2
CB	ADDB	"	2	2
CC	LDD	"	3	3
CE	LDU	"	3	3
DØ	SUBB	DIRECT	4	2
D1	CMPB	"	4	2
D2	SBCB	"	4	2
D3	ADDD	"	6	2
D4	ANDB	"	4	2
D5	BITB	"	4	2
D6	LDB	"	4	2

OP	MNEM	MODE	~	#
D7	STB	DIRECT	4	2
D8	EORB	"	4	2
D9	ADCB	"	4	2
DA	ORB	"	4	2
DB	ADDB	"	4	2
DC	LDD	"	5	2
DD	STD	"	5	2
DE	LDU	"	5	2
DF	STU	"	5	2
EØ	SUBB	INDEXED	4	2
E1	CMPB	"	4	2
E2	SBCB	"	4	2
E3	ADDD	"	6	2
E4	ANDB	"	4	2
E5	BITB	"	4	2
E6	LDB	"	4	2
E7	STB	"	4	2
E8	EORB	"	4	2

OP	MNEM	MODE	~	#
E9	ADCB	INDEXED	4	2
EA	ORB	"	4	2
EB	ADDB	"	4	2
EC	LDD	"	5	2
ED	STD	"	5	2
EE	LDU	"	5	2
EF	STU	"	5	2
FØ	SUBB	EXTENDED	5	3
F1	CMPB	"	5	3
F2	SBCB	"	5	3
F3	ADDD	"	7	3
F4	ANDB	"	5	3
F5	BITB	"	5	3
F6	LDB	"	5	3
F7	STB	"	5	3
F8	EORB	"	5	3
F9	ADCB	"	5	3
FA	ORB	"	5	3

OP	MNEM	MODE	~	#
FB	ADDB	EXTENDED	5	3
FC	LDD	"	6	3
FD	STD	"	6	3
FE	LDU	"	6	3
FF	STU	"	6	3
1021	LBRN	RELATIVE	5	4
1022	LBHI	"	5(6)	4
1023	LBLS	"	5(6)	4
1024	LBHS/LBCC	"	5(6)	4
1025	LBCS/LBLO	"	5(6)	4
1026	LBNE	"	5(6)	4
1027	LBEQ	"	5(6)	4
1028	LBVC	"	5(6)	4
1029	LBVS	"	5(6)	4
102A	LBPL	"	5(6)	4
102B	LBMI	"	5(6)	4
102C	LBGE	"	5(6)	4
102D	LBLT	"	5(6)	4

OP	MNEM	MODE	~	#
102E	LBGT	RELATIVE	5(6)	4
102F	LBLE	"	5(6)	4
103F	SWI2	INHERENT	20	2
1083	CMPD	IMMED	5	4
108C	CMPY	"	5	4
108E	LDY	"	4	4
1093	CMPD	DIRECT	7	3
109C	CMPY	"	7	3
109E	LDY	"	6	3
109F	STY	"	6	3
10A3	CMPD	INDEXED	7	3
10AC	CMPY	"	7	3
10AE	LDY	"	6	3
10AF	STY	"	6	3
10B3	CMPD	EXTENDED	8	4
10BC	CMPY	"	8	4
10BE	LDY	"	7	4
10BF	STY	"	7	4

OP	MNEM	MODE	~	#
10CE	LDS	IMMED	4	4
10DE	LDS	DIRECT	6	3
10DF	STS	"	6	3
10EE	LDS	INDEXED	6	3
10EF	STS	"	6	3
10FE	LDS	EXTENDED	7	4
10FF	STS	"	7	4
113F	SWI3	INHERENT	20	2
1183	CMPU	IMMED	5	4
118C	CMPS	"	5	4
1193	CMPU	DIRECT	7	3
119C	CMPS	"	7	3
11A3	CMPU	INDEXED	7	3
11AC	CMPS	"	7	3
11B3	CMPU	EXTENDED	8	4
11BC	CMPS	"	8	4

Machine code register

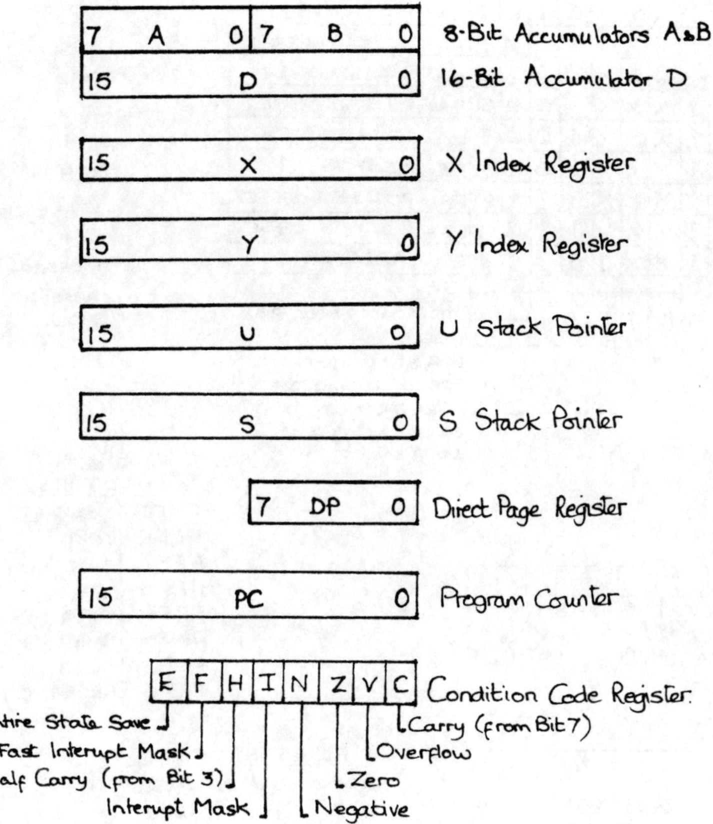

INDEXED ADDRESSING POST-BYTE
REGISTER BIT ASSIGNMENTS

POST-BYTE REGISTER BIT								INDEXED ADDRESSING MODE
7	6	5	4	3	2	1	0	
0	X	X	X	X	X	X	X	EA=,R ± 4 BIT OFFSET
1	X	X	0	0	0	0	0	,R+
1	X	X	X	0	0	0	1	,R++
1	X	X	0	0	0	1	0	,-R
1	X	X	X	0	0	1	1	,--R
1	X	X	X	0	1	0	0	EA=,R ± 0 OFFSET
1	X	X	X	0	1	0	1	EA=,R ±ACCB OFFSET
1	X	X	X	0	1	1	0	EA=,R ±ACCA OFFSET
1	X	X	X	1	0	0	0	EA=,R ± 7 BIT OFFSET
1	X	X	X	1	0	0	1	EA=,R ± 15 BIT OFFSET
1	X	X	X	1	0	1	1	EA=,R ± D OFFSET
1	X	X	X	1	1	0	0	EA=,PC ± 7 BIT OFFSET
1	X	X	X	1	1	0	1	EA=,PC ± 15 BIT OFFSET
1	X	X	1	1	1	1	1	EA=,ADDRESS

ADDRESSING MODE FIELD

I FIELD
FOR B7 =1 : INDIRECT
FOR B7 = 0 : SIGN BIT

REGISTER FIELD
00 : R = X   01 : R = Y
10 : R = U   11 : R = S

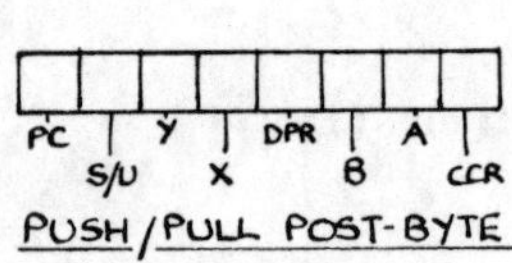

PUSH/PULL POST-BYTE

SOURCE	DESTINATION

TRANSFER/EXCHANGE
POST-BYTE

6809
STACKING ORDER

PULL ORDER
↓
CC
A
B
DP
X Hi
X Lo
Y Hi
Y Lo
U/S Hi
U/S Lo
PC Hi
PC Lo
↑
PUSH ORDER

INCREASING
MEMORY
↓

6809
VECTORS

FFFE	RESTART
FFFC	NMI
FFFA	SWI
FFF8	IRQ
FFF6	FIRQ
FFF4	SWI2
FFF2	SWI3
FFF0	RESERVED

REGISTER FIELD.

0000 = D (A:B)		0101 = PC	
0001 = X		1000 = A	
0010 = Y		1001 = B	
0011 = U		1010 = CCR	
0100 = S		1011 = DPR	

Memory map

```
=================================================================
= Location    Description                                      =
= Hex                                                          =
=================================================================
=                                                              =
= 0019        Address of start of BASIC program               =
= 001A        Address of end of BASIC program                 =
= 001B        Address of start of variable storage            =
= 001D        Address of start of array storage               =
= 001F        Address of start of free memory                 =
= 0021        Address of start of string stack                =
= 0023        Address of upper limit of BASIC                 =
= 0027        Address of highest available RAM                =
= 006C        Current cursor column position                  =
= 006F        Holds current device number                     =
= 0071        Warm start flag                                 =
= 0072        Warm start vector                               =
= 0074        Address of highest memory address               =
= 007C        Block type                                      =
= 007D        Number of bytes to be put out                   =
= 007E/F      Base address of bytes                           =
= 0080        Checksum                                        =
= 0081        Error code                                      =
= 0088        Point to next location for screen output        =
= 0089        Ditto                                           =
= 008C        Sound frequency                                 =
= 008D        Duration of sound                               =
= 008F        Blink count                                     =
= 0090/91     Leader byte count for tapes                     =
= 0095/96     Cassette motor delay                            =
= 0099        Line printer field width                        =
= 009A        Last field width                                =
= 009B        Line printer width                              =
= 009C        Print head position for line printer            =
= 009D        Transfer address after CLOAD                     =
= 00B6        Holds current PMODE                             =
= 0100        SWI 3 vector                                    =
= 0103        SWI 2 vector                                    =
= 0106        SWI 1 vector                                    =
= 0109        NMI vector                                      =
= 010C        IRQ vector                                      =
= 010F        FIRQ vector                                     =
= 0121        Points to BASIC command token table             =
= 0123        As above for jump table                         =
= 0126        As above for function token table               =
= 0128        As above for function jump table                =
= 0148        Buffer full auto line feed flag                 =
= 0149        Alpha lock flag                                 =
= 014A        Number of chars. to be printed in end of line   =
= 014B        Perform carriage return to printer              =
= 014C        Perform line feed                               =
= 014D        Redundant                                       =
= 014E        Redundant                                       =
=                                                              =
=================================================================
```

```
=====================================================================
= Location    Description                                           =
= Hex                                                               =
=====================================================================
=                                                                   =
= 0151        Start of keyboard rollover table                      =
= 0152-159    Covers entire keyboard                                =
= 015A        Left joystick X position                              =
= 015B        Left joystick Y position                              =
= 015C        Right joystick X position                             =
= 015D        Right joystick Y position                             =
= 01D2        Cassette file name                                    =
= 01D4        Cassette file buffer                                  =
= 01E5        Transfer address used by CSAVEM                       =
= 0200-3FFF   Buffer for cassettes etc.                             =
= 0400-5FFF   Text screen default area                              =
= 0600-07FF   Graphics screen/program/variable storage             =
= 0C00-7FFF   User RAM, depending on graphics pages                 =
= 8006        Poll keyboard                                         =
= 8009        Blink cursor                                          =
= 800C        Write character to text screen                        =
= 800F        Ditto for line printer (char. in A as above)          =
= 8012        Update joystick readings                              =
= 8015        Turn on cassette relay                                =
= 8018        Turn off cassette relay                               =
= 801B        Prepare cassette for writing                          =
= 801E        Shove byte to cassette from A                         =
= 8021        Prepare cassette for data                             =
= 8024        Returns next byte in A                                =
= 8027        Gets next bit in from cassette                        =
= 8033        BASIC command word table                             =
= 8154        BASIC command jump table                             =
= 81CA        BASIC function word table                            =
= 8250        BASIC function jump table                            =
= 82A9        BASIC error message table                            =
= 82E0        BASIC interpreter                                    =
= C000-FEFF   Cartridge slot                                        =
= FF00        PIA                                                   =
= FFF2        SWI 3 vector                                          =
= FFF4        SWI 2 vector                                          =
= FFF6        FIRQ vector                                           =
= FFF8        IRQ vector                                            =
= FFFA        SWI 1 vector                                          =
= FFFC        NMI vector                                            =
= FFFE        Reset vector                                          =
=                                                                   =
=====================================================================
```

Memory architecture

Decimal Address	Contents	Hex Address
Ø – 1Ø23	System Work Area	Ø - 3FF
1Ø24 - 1535	Text Screen	4ØØ - 5FF
1536 - 3Ø71	Graphic – page 1	6ØØ - BFF
3Ø72 - 46Ø7	" " 2	CØØ - 11FF
46Ø8 - 6143	" " 3	12ØØ - 17FF
6144 - 7679	" " 4	18ØØ - 1DFF
768Ø - 9215	" " 5	1EØØ - 23FF
9216 - 1Ø751	" " 6	24ØØ - 29FF
1Ø752 - 12287	" " 7	2AØØ - 2FFF
12288 - 13823	" " 8	3ØØØ - 35FF
13824 - 37767	Program & Variables - user's	36ØØ - 7FFF
37768 - 49151	BASIC ROM	8ØØØ - BFFF
49152 - 65279	Cartridge Port	CØØØ - FEFF
6528Ø - 65535	Input / Output	FFØØ - FFFF

Powers tables

```
Powers of  2                       Powers of  16
-----------                        ------------

         N                                  N
         2        N                         16                       N
------------------------           --------------------------------------
       256        8                                      1            0
       512        9                                     16            1
     1,024       10                                    256            2
     2,048       11                                  4,096            3
     4,096       12                                 65,536            4
     8,192       13                              1,048,576            5
    16,384       14                             16,777,216            6
    32,768       15                            268,435,456            7
    65,536       16                          4,294,967,296            8
   131,072       17                         68,719,476,736            9
   262,144       18                      1,099,511,627,776           10
   524,288       19                     17,592,186,044,416           11
 1,048,576       20                    281,474,976,710,656           12
 2,097,152       21                  4,503,599,627,370,496           13
 4,194,304       22                 72,057,594,037,927,936           14
 8,388,608       23              1,152,921,504,606,846,976           15
16,777,216       24
```

Printer port

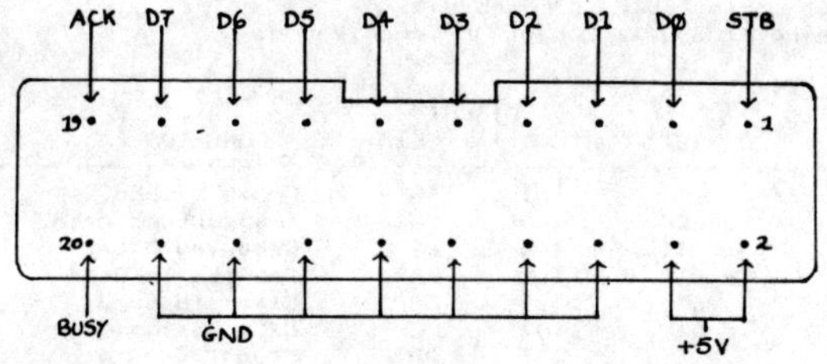

RS232 standards

<pre>
                        EIA RS232-C (CCITT V24)

        Notes

        Transmission is serial (asynchronous).
        MARK = binary 1 = OFF = -3 to -25 volts.
        SPACE = binary 0 = ON = +3 to +25 volts.
        25-pin "D" type connector.
        Data Control Equipment (DCE) has female connector.
        Data Terminal Equipment (DTE) has male connector.
        Open circuit drive voltage cannot exceed 25 volts.
        Terminator resistance 3-7K ohms.
        50 foot maximum DCE, DTE separation.
        2500 pico farad max conductor capacitance.
</pre>

| | | | CIRCUIT | | |
PIN	NAME	DIRECTION	CCITT	EIA	FUNCTION
01	FG	-	101	AA	Frame Ground.
02	TD	To DCE	103	BA	Transmitted Data.
03	RD	To DTE	104	BB	Received Data.
04	RTS	To DCE	105	CA	Request To Send.
05	CTS	To DTE	106	CB	Clear To Send.
06	DSR	To DTE	107	CC	Data Set Ready.
07	SG	-	102	AB	Signal Ground.
08	DCD	To DTE	109	CF	Data Carrier Detect.
09		To DTE			Positive DC Test Voltage.
10		To DTE			Negative DC Test Voltage.
11	QM	To DTE	Bell	208A	Equaliser Mode.
12	(S)DCD	To DTE	122	SCF	Secondary Data Carrier Detect.
13	(S)CTS	To DTE	121	SCB	Secondary Clear To Send.
14	(S)TD	To DCE	118	SBA	Secondary Transmitted Data.
	NS	To DCE	Bell	208A	New Synch.
15	TC	To DTE	114	DB	Transmitter Clock.
16	(S)RD	To DTE	119	SBB	Secondary Received Data.
	DCT	To DTE	Bell	208A	Divided Clock Transmitter.
17	RC	To DTE	115	DD	Receiver Clock.
18	DCR	To DTE	Bell	208A	Divided Clock Receiver.
19	(S)RTS	To DCE	120	SCA	Secondary Request to Send.
20	DTR	To DCE	108.2	CD	Data Terminal Ready.
21	SQ	To DTE	110	CG	Signal Quality Detect.
22	RI	To DTE	125	CE	Ring Indicator.
23		To DCE	111	CH	Data Rate Selector.
		To DTE	112	CI	Data Rate Selector.
24	TC	To DCE	113	DA	EXT Transmitter Clock.
25		To DCE	Bell	113B	Busy.

CCITT V24 Circuit Definitions

Circuit 102 - Signal Ground or Common Return

This conductor establishes the signal common return for
interchange circuits.

Circuit 103 - Transmitted Data

The data signals originated by the DTE, to be transmitted
via the data channel to one or more remote data stations,
are transferred on this circuit to DCE.

Circuit 104 - Received Data

The data signals generated by the DCE, in response to data
channel line signals received from a remote data station,
are transferred on this circuit to the DTE.

Circuit 105 - Request to Send

Controls the data channel transmit function of the DCE.

Circuit 106 - Ready for Sending

Indicates whether the DCE is conditioned to transmit data on
the data channel.

Circuit 107 - Data Set Ready

Indicates whether the DCE is ready to operate.

Circuit 108/1 - Connect Data Set to Line

Controls switching of the signal-conversion or similar
equipment to or from the line.

Circuit 108/2 - Data Terminal Ready

Controls switching of the signal-conversion or similar
equipment to or from the line.

Circuit 109 - Carrier Detect

Indicates whether the received data channel line signal is
within appropriate limits, as specified by the relevant
recommendation for DCE.

Circuit 110 - Data Signal Quality Detector

Indicates whether there is a reasonable probability of an

error in the data received on the data channel.

Circuit 111 - Data Signalling Rate Selector

Used to select one or two data signalling rates of a
dual-rate synchronous DCE, or to select one of the two
ranges of data signalling rates of a dual-range synchronous
DCE.

Circuit 112 - Data Signalling Rate Selector

Used to select one of the two data signalling rates or
ranges of rates in the DTE to coincide with the data
signalling rate or range of rates in use in a dual-rate
synchronous or dual-range asynchronous DCE.

Circuit 113 - Transmitter Signal Element Timing

Provides the DCE with signal element timing information.

Circuit 114 - Transmitter Signal Element Timing

Provides the DTE with signal element timing information.

Circuit 115 - Receiver Signal Element Timing

Provides the DTE with signal element timing information.

Circuit 116 - Select Standby

Used to select the normal or standby facilities such as
signal convertors and communication channels.

Circuit 117 - Standby Indicator

Indicates whether the DCE is conditioned in its standby mode
with the pre-determined facilities replaced by their
reserves.

Circuit 118 - Transmitted Backward Channel Data

Equivalent to circuit 103, except that it is used for data
received on the backward channel.

Circuit 120 - Transmit Backward Channel Line Signal

Equivalent to circuit 105, except that it is used to control
the backward channel transmit function of the DCE.

Circuit 121 - Backward Channel Ready

Equivalent to circuit 106, except that it is used to

indicate whether the DCE is conditioned to transmit data on
the backward channel.

Circuit 122 - Supervisory Carrier Detect

Equivalent to circuit 109, except that it is used to
indicate whether the received backward channel line signal
is within appropriate limits.

Circuit 123 - Backward Channel Signal Quality Detector

Equivalent to circuit 110, except that it is used to
indicate the signal quality of the received backward channel
line signal.

Circuit 124 - Select Frequency Groups

Used to select the desired frequency groups available on the
DCE.

Circuit 125 - Calling Indicator

Indicates whether a calling signal is being received by the
DCE.

Circuit 126 - Select Transmit Frequency

Used to select the required transmit frequency of the DCE.

Circuit 127 - Select Receive Frequency

Used to select the required receive frequency of the DCE.

Circuit 128 - Receiver Signal Element Timing

Provides the DCE with signal element timing information.

Circuit 129 - Request to Receive

Used to control the receive function of the DCE.

Circuit 130 - Transmit Backward Tone

Controls the transmission of a backward channel tone.

Circuit 131 - Received Character Timing

Provides the DTE with character timing information.

Circuit 132 - Return to Non-Data Mode

Used to restore the non-data mode provided with the DCE, without releasing the line connection to the remote station.

Circuit 133 - Ready for Receiving

Controls the transfer of data on circuit 104, indicating whether the DTE is capable of accepting a given amount of data, specified in the appropriate recommendation for intermediate equipment, for example, error control equipment.

Circuit 134 - Received Data Present

Used to separate information messages from supervisory messages, transferred on circuit 104.

Circuit 191 - Transmitted Voice Answer

Signals generated by a voice answer unit in the DTE are transferred on this circuit to the DCE.

Circuit 192 - Received Voice Answer

Received voice signals, generated by a voice answering unit at the remote data terminal, are transferred on this circuit to the DTE.

Other CCITT "V" Interfaces

V10

Electrical characteristics for unbalanced double-current interchange circuits for general use with integrated circuit equipment in the field of data communications.

V11

Electrical characteristics for balanced double-current interchange circuits for general use with integrated circuit equipment in the field of data communications.

V15

Use of acoustic coupling for data transmission.

V16

Medical analogue data transmission modems.

V19

Modems for parallel data transmission using telephone signalling frequencies.

V20

Parallel data transmission modems standardised for universal use in the general switch telephone network.

V21

200-baud modem standardised for use in the general switched telephone network.

V22

Defines the procedures and standards for 1200 baud full duplex communications over the public switched network.

V23

600/1200-baud modem standardised for use in the general switched telephone network.

V24

List of definitions for interchange circuits between data terminal equipment and data circuit terminating equipment.

V25

Automatic calling and/or answering equipment on the general switched telephone network, including disabling of echo-suppressors on manually established calls.

V26

2400 bits per second modem standardised for use on 4-wire leased telephone-type circuits.

V26 (alternative)

2400/1200 bits per second modem standardised for use in the general switched telephone network.

V27

4800 bits per second modems with manual equaliser standardised for use on leased telephone-type circuits.

V27 (alternative 1)

4800 bits per second modems with automatic equaliser

standardised for use on leased telephone-type circuits.

V27 (alternative 2)

4800/2400 bits per second modems standardised for use in the
general switched telephone network.

V28

Electrical characteristics for unbalanced   double-current
interchange circuits.

V29

9600 bits per second modems standardised for use in leased
telephone circuits.

V31

Electrical characteristics for single current interchange
circuits controlled by contact closure.

V35

Data transmission at 48 kilobits per second using 60-108 KHz
group band circuits.

V36

Modems for synchronous transmission using 60-108 KHz group
band circuits.

Useful hints and tips

This section is a collection of Dragon miscellanea gleaned over the months. It contains material that we have discovered by ourselves, or seen in various magazines, or even overheard in casual conversation at computer shows, user groups, etc.

It just goes to show how much undocumented information there is floating around about the Dragon, and, even more, how much there is still to be discovered. The publishers would be grateful to hear of any Dragon fact or figure that you've discovered, with a view to sharing this knowledge with everyone else in future publications.

But now, without further ado, and without any concern for presenting things in a logical order (see the index if you get totally lost!), let's start with a few USR functions.

USR functions

As is usual with the Dragon manual, these have been wrongly described. Most people redefine USR0 over and over again, and just use that one for several different reasons. However, USR1 to USR9 can all equally well be used, provided that the call in a Basic program is prefixed by a 0. That is, use A = USR01(A) (for example), rather than USR1(A). For example:

```
10 DEFUSR8=&H8015:REM START OF M/C ROUTINE TO
   TURN THE CASSETTE MOTOR ON
20 DEFUSR9=&H8018:REM START OF M/C ROUTINE TO
   TURN THE CASSETTE MOTOR OFF AGAIN
30 A$=INKEY$: IFA$=""THEN30
40 IFA$="*"THENA=USR08(A):GOTO30
50 IFA$="@"THENA=USR09(A):GOTO30
60 GOTO30
```

All this little demonstration does is to turn the cassette motor on if the '*' key is pressed, and turn it off if the '@' key is pressed. No other key has any effect.

Speeded up Dragon

The POKE to speed up the Dragon is well known (POKE 65495,0), but unfortunately doesn't work on all Dragons. However, there are other ways to speed up certain functions. For instance, INKEY$ is not the fastest of functions, and in a program that requires the user to enter one of the four arrow keys to move a character about on the screen, you might like to use the following four memory locations instead:

For up arrow, read PEEK(341).
For down arrow, read PEEK(342)
For left arrow, read PEEK(343).
For right arrow, read PEEK(344).

These locations return a 255 if the relevant key is not being pressed, but if it is, a value of 223 is put into that location. Thus, by using:

IFPEEK(344)=223THEN move the character up

we can easily handle those four particular keys.

There are some other (safe!) locations in the Dragon that can be POKEd in order to speed things up a little. For instance, if you want to increase the processing speed of your Dragon, try the following:

POKE &HFFD7,0
POKE &HFFD9,0

The second in conjunction with the first should be safe on all Dragons (it is on ours!). To get things back to normal again, use:

POKE &HFFD8,0
POKE &HFFD6,0

And more on INKEY$

As we all know, unless specific steps are taken to disable the break key, pressing this will break into a loop that is waiting for a key to be pressed. However, by using the internal routine that handles the INKEY$ function, a program will be seen to be behaving as normal, but will however be inaccessible to people typing BREAK.

Thus, we might have something like:

```
10 PRINT"PRESS ANY KEY TO CONTINUE":EXEC41994
```

This just calls up the internal routine to handle INKEY$.

NEW programs for OLD Dragons

We've mentioned elsewhere in this book that typing in NEW <ENTER> doesn't remove everything from memory, but merely resets internal pointers so that the program can no longer be accessed.

Therefore, it ought to be possible to retrieve a program that has been accidentally NEWed. Provided that no new program lines are entered, no new variables are assigned (and someone hasn't switched the machine off!), the following short program will do the trick.

```
100 CLEAR 200,32749
110 Y=32749
120 DATA 158,25,189.131.48.2,159,27,159.29,159,31,57
130 FORI=1TO14:READX:POKEY+I,X:NEXT
```

This program should always be sitting in your Dragon, and to execute it when you've accidentally said goodbye to a program, use EXEC 32750.

Loading information

As we've seen, the two hex locations &8015 and &8018 (decimal 32789 and 32792 respectively) can be used to turn the cassette motor on and off. There is a third useful location when dealing with cassette decks, and this is the one which handles the CLOADing of a BASIC program.

If you aren't fussed about what filename you're looking for on tape, try EXEC 46800.

Another point about loading programs, is that it is always a good idea to leave a gap between stuff on tape whether it be programs or data. This is usually done with the MOTORON and MOTOROFF commands, but if entered in direct mode, MOTOROFF can take some time to type, thus leaving an inordinately long gap on the tape.

Even worse, you might spell the word incorrectly and leave an extremely long gap as you try to delete characters to get it right! To achieve the same effect as MOTOROFF, just generate a syntax error. For example:

H <ENTER>

HEX/DEC and OCT

We're all familiar with the fact that the Dragon can handle decimal as well as hexadecimal numbers.

Well, it can also handle octal numbers, by replacing the &H characters with &O.

Thus:

PRINT &O number

will return the decimal equivalent of the octal number 'number'.

Screen information

The largest part of this book is devoted to the handling of graphics, but even armed with all that knowledge there is a surprising amount of uncharted material concerned with displaying information on the screen.

For instance, to simulate a mixture of text and graphics on the screen, a simple way in BASIC would be simply to switch from one to the other very rapidly. Even better, if your machine can handle the'speed up' POKE the display will appear relatively flicker free.

Of course, the ultimate goal would be to write this sort of thing in machine code, but as a small BASIC demonstration, how about this:

```
100 PMODE1,1:COLOURO,5:REM POKE65495,O IF YOUR
    MACHINE CAN HANDLE IT!
110 PCLS:CIRCLE (125,100),80
120 SCREEN1
130 FORI=1TO10:NEXTI
140 SCREENO
150 FORI=1TO10:NEXTI
160 GOTO120
```

All this does is draw a circle on a high resolution screen, and then swap from that to the screen displaying the listing.

And more

This is to be used when you require an increase in the normal colour resolution available.

It is possible, in PMODE3, to fool the Dragon into displaying all 256 character positions at a time, which makes pixels overlap. This effectively doubles the resolution, although it does make it very difficult to control the colour. Still, it's probably worth the attempt:

```
100 PMODE3:SCREEN1,0:PCLS
110 PMODE4,1
120 CIRCLE (128,96),96
130 PAINT (128,96)
140 A$=INKEY$: IFA$=""THEN140
```

Run this program as normal, and then delete line 110 to see what kind of effect you can really get out of the Dragon!

And yet more!

In our highest resolution graphics mode, you can normally only display two colours at a time. However, it is possible to get a purple haze on the screen, with the aid of one POKE.

```
10 PMODE3,1:SCREEN1,1:POKE65314,248
```

By doing this, BASIC thinks that you're in four-colour mode, while the video chip is still convinced that you're in two-colour high resolution mode.

Our new colour set now has the values of 2 = light purple, 1 = black and 0 = white.

Let's take a break

We mentioned earlier that there is a way to get around the problem of people BREAKing into Dragon programs while the program sits and waits for a key to be pressed. This involved using an internal routine to collect the key being pressed.

A more unsubtle, but equally effective way, would be to disable the BREAK key totally, so that pressing it would have no effect at all.

To do that, enter the following in direct mode:

```
POKE 411,228
POKE 412,203
POKE 413,4
POKE 414,237
POKE 415,228
```

Once that little piece of code is sitting in the machine, the BREAK key can be disabled by:

```
POKE 410,236
```

and re-enabled with

```
POKE 410,57
```

Back to loading

It is possible, using the CLOADM and CSAVEM commands, to load and save screen images to and from cassette, which could be used to enhance certain programs considerably.

To do this, we need to know where the screen pages are stored in memory, and in order they sit at:

Page No.	Hexadecimal address
0	0600-0BFF
1	0C00-11FF
2	1200-17FF
3	1800-1DFF
4	1E00-23FF
5	2400-29FF
6	2A00-2FFF
7	3000-35FF

On top of this, we need to know that:

PMODE0   uses 1 page.
PMODE1/2   uses 2 pages.
PMODE3/4   uses 4 pages.

CLOADM is obviously the command required to re-load a previously CSAVEMed file, but where to save from?

Assuming for the sake of argument that you're starting with page 1, the following table shows the locations to save:

PMODE   Command

---

0   CSAVEM ''fred'',&H600,&HBFF,&H600
1 or 2   CSAVEM ''fred'',&H600,&H11FF,&H600
3 or 4   CSAVEM ''fred'',&H600,&H1DFF,&H600

And finally

To round things off, just a few words about GET and PUT. The Dragon manual treats these in a very disdainful manner, and indeed would seem to suggest that the largest screen area that could be GOT (why don't BASIC keywords have past and future tenses?!) and PUT anywhere, in the highest resolution mode, is about 80 by 75 pixels. Not a great deal.

However, all we need to know about any pixel in the highest resolution screen (just 2 colours to play with, remember) is whether that pixel is on or off. Thus one byte can store information about 8 different pixels.

Therefore, to read an entire screen in PMODE4 requires some (256*192)/8 bytes, or 6K. If you believed the manual, it would require almost a quarter of a million bytes!

The following program demonstrates this technique by reading an entire screen (which does take a little while in BASIC), waiting for a key to be pressed, and then PUTting it back to the screen again.

```
100 PMODE4:PCLS:SCREEN1,0
110 FORI=1TO191STEP2:FORJ=1TO255STEP2:PSET(J,I):
    NEXTJ,I
120 DIM A(1250)
130 GET (0,0)-(255,191),A,G:REM SAVE FULL GRAPHIC
    DETAIL
140 PCLS
150 A$=INKEY$:IFA$=""THEN150
160 PUT (0,0)-(255,191),A,PSET
170 A$=INKEY$:IFA$=""THEN170
```

So, using this technique, 2 or 3 pages can be saved in BASIC, and still leave room for a reasonable program to manipulate it all.

Index